THE TRUTH ABOUT JESUS

The Truth about Jesus

Edited by

DONALD ARMSTRONG

WILLIAM B. EERDMANS PUBLISHING COMPANY
GRAND RAPIDS, MICHIGAN / CAMBRIDGE, U.K.

© 1998 Wm. B. Eerdmans Publishing Co.
255 Jefferson Ave. S.E., Grand Rapids, Michigan 49503 /
P.O. Box 163, Cambridge CB3 9PU U.K.

Printed in the United States of America

03 02 01 00 99 98   7 6 5 4 3 2 1

Library of Congress Cataloging-in-Publication Data

The truth about Jesus / edited by Donald Armstrong
      p.   cm.
   Papers presented at a meeting.
   Includes bibliographical references.
   ISBN 0-8028-3855-3 (alk. paper)
   1. Jesus Christ — Person and offices — Congresses.   2. Anglican
Communion — Congresses.   I. Armstrong, Donald, III.
BT205.T774   1998
232 — dc21   97-51673
                                                      CIP

Contents

Preface: The Truth about Jesus

THE ESSAYS CONTAINED in this book, *The Truth about Jesus,* are the edited addresses given at our fourth annual Anglican Institute Conference, held in Birmingham, Alabama, in April of 1997. Previous Anglican Institute Conferences held in Colorado Springs — The Practice of Anglicanism (1993), The Reconstruction of a Vital Via Media (1994), and Unashamed Anglicanism (1996) — join The Truth about Jesus Conference as vehicles for the promotion of a vibrant, historic Christianity in the Anglican Tradition. The impressive list of contributors to this volume indicates the wide-ranging and serious efforts of the Institute to consider topics of core importance to the life of faith. By bringing together the finest minds in the church, the Institute offers a forum for significant theological reflection.

In an age of chaos and uncertainty in both the church and the culture, an effective faith rooted in a sturdy tradition is desperately needed. Not being engaged in the ever-changing and symptomatic temporal issues, the Anglican Institute is positioned to help reclaim the church's historic identity and spiritual focus, in the hope that it may be a vehicle for the mighty works of God. The Truth about Jesus is a significant contribution to the accomplishment of this task.

It is our purpose to ground our work in the formational historic events — the Incarnation, Crucifixion, Resurrection of Christ, and the coming of the Holy Spirit — combined with the tolerance, fair-mindedness, and generosity that have long marked our Anglican way — to fortify and proclaim the Apostolic Christian faith of the church — expressed in Scripture, interpreted in the creeds, guarded by tradition, and experienced in sacrament.

The work of the Anglican Institute has been greatly supported over the years by the generosity of the St. Louis Board of the Institute, and the vestry, staff, and parish of Grace Episcopal Church in Colorado Springs — especially Cheryl Vossekuil, Sharon Fasano, Dareleen Schaffer, Shirley Waddill, and Bud Libengood. The Bishop of South Carolina, the Rt. Rev. Edward L. Salmon, the Rev. C. Frederick Barbee, Executive Director, Jessie H. Armstrong, Institute Administrator, and the Rev. Linda K. Seracuse, Vicar of Grace Church, have worked with clarity and diligence over the years to continue this most important work. A special thanks must be given to Betty Gouraud, whose generosity has significantly underwritten the Institute, enabling it to greatly expand the effectiveness and reach of its work. I also wish to thank the Rev. Dr. Alister McGrath for his theological advice and counsel in the design and substance of our conferences.

The Rev. Donald Armstrong

Introduction: The Truth about Jesus

MEDIA INTEREST CONCERNING the "Jesus Seminar" and a "new quest for the historical Jesus" have occasioned considerable unease among Christians of all traditions. As any holy season approaches, we can count on cover stories in all the weekly news magazines containing the latest deconstructionist interpretation of the revelation of Holy Scripture. If one is a parish priest, he or she can count on being handed countless copies of these articles by parishioners thinking they have discovered something worth reading and hoping to keep their pastor up-to-date by passing it along.

One reason the "new thinking" about Jesus has captured the imagination of so many cultural chaplains and religious seekers is the ease with which a low-demand, nonjudgmental gospel is accepted by postmodern people. Such "scholarship" nestles Jesus safely away doing his father's work with no interference in our present worldly preoccupations and distractions. What could be a more convenient and marketable God for an age when humanity's desire is to be in charge, to have it their way?

What can and should be said about this "new thinking" to a world being seduced by such clever but faulty interpretations of the revelation of God in Jesus Christ? What can we really know about Jesus of Nazareth as he actually was? Is the Christ of faith the same as the man from Galilee? Can we match what we *know* about him with what we *believe* about him? Is he *the* way, *the* truth, and *the* life, or merely, as many believe today even within the church, simply "*a* way, *a* truth, *a* life?

In planning the conference that brought forth the essays contained in this book, the leadership of the Anglican Institute wanted to offer a reasoned and viable alternative to this sketchy and market-driven

1

thinking. We were particularly worried about the steady drift toward an understanding of a Jesus who is not fully divine. Clearly the Jesus of traditional biblical teaching needed to be reasserted in a compelling and positive way before nonscholarly liberalism had him seated right next to us in the pew searching for salvation.

The edited conference lectures that comprise this book engage precisely this issue of the truth about Jesus. The scholars who wrote these presentations were requested not simply to react to the latest trends in speculative theology, but to proclaim the sturdy and durable Jesus of Scripture, tradition, and reason within the context of a worshipping community, a community in which the same risen Lord could be truly present and revealing.

It was clear to us that such a task could not be tackled by lazy minds grasping for a synthetic faith. We did not want, in the end, to be left with a Saviour who simply affirms us because we had not been willing to put forth the effort to learn, appropriate, and subject ourselves to those things necessary for salvation. So we gathered together some of the most alert and active voices in the church to present their most faithful work on this urgent issue.

Written by a faculty of scholars from around the Anglican Communion, these essays explore and critique the current "quest for the historic Jesus." But rather than just reacting to this so-called quest, rather than inveighing against feeble theological thinking, these works proclaim afresh the Jesus of scriptural understanding and firmly address his ultimate, unique, and absolute significance for our times. In the midst of the uncertainty, confusion, doubt, and insecurity so rampant in the church today, here at last is a clear, faithful, and proclaimable understanding of God as revealed in Jesus Christ, one that will stand up to the rigors of postmodern life and thought.

The Rev. Dr. N. T. Wright, Dean of Lichfield Cathedral, offers us a scholarly overview and critique of current Jesus study. In a work that is foundational for any reflection on Jesus at the end of the twentieth century, Dr. Wright reasserts the compelling biblical truth about Jesus.

The Rev. Dr. Alister McGrath, Principal of Wycliffe Hall, Oxford, reflects on Jesus as "the way, the truth, and the life" in relation to other religious beliefs. This timely and thoughtful essay considers Christianity's claim for the uniqueness of Jesus in a cultural atmosphere where every claim is considered to be equally true.

The Rev. Fleming Rutledge, popular preacher and theologian in the American church, writes with technical precision but with an application one might call "the Bible and the *New York Times*" of Jesus and his saving work. To be a disciple means allowing one's own identity to be determined by the identity of the one who died forsaken on the cross.

The Rev. Dr. Walter Eversley of Virginia Theological Seminary examines the Jesus of history as reflected in a wide cross-section of cultural images and art. He perceptively shows the universal truth and relevance of Jesus in an age when diversity of truths is all the rage.

With great anecdotal wisdom, The Rt. Rev. Edward Salmon, Bishop of South Carolina, shares the reality of Jesus at work within his church. This essay is an inspirational witness to the presence of the risen Lord and a call to discipleship that is both sacrificial and life-giving. Bishop Salmon's diagnosis and prescription for the health of the church should be taken seriously. The reality of Jesus in the life of the Christian community is apparent in the central sacrament of the church, as examined by The Rev. Dr. John Koenig of General Theological Seminary, and in the church's call to ministry, as explored by The Rev. Dr. Guy Lytle, Dean of St. Luke's School of Theology at Sewanee.

In the final presentation, The Rev. Dr. Diogenes Allen of Princeton Theological Seminary offers a well-developed and impassioned description of the experience of a relationship with the living Lord who comes to us to make himself known to our hearts and minds. This, at last, brings the Jesus of history into our personal histories and raises our souls into the presence of God in heaven.

The epilogue is by The Rev. Dr. Gareth Jones, University of Wales, who was the Conference Preacher and Chaplain.

In a time when so many are succumbing to the "holy man" idea of a Jesus who makes little or no difference, the essays in this volume reaffirm and articulate the Christ of Holy Scripture who reveals the very nature of the Father, who shows us the path to everlasting joy, and whose death on the cross accomplished our salvation.

The Rev. Donald Armstrong
Rector, The Anglican Institute
London, England
23 October 1997

Jesus and the Quest

N. T. WRIGHT

1. Introduction

I believe that the historical quest for Jesus is a necessary and non-negotiable aspect of Christian discipleship; that we in our generation have a chance to be renewed in discipleship and mission precisely by means of this quest; and, even, that we in the Anglican Communion may have a chance to play a significant role in this quest. However, as you would expect from anything that is heavy with potential for the kingdom of God, there are huge problems and even dangers within the quest, and I would like to say something about them here.[1]

Right from the start there are pitfalls in even addressing the subject, and we may as well be clear about them. It is desperately easy, when among like-minded friends, to become complacent. We continually hear of wild new theories about Jesus. Every month or two some publisher comes up with a blockbuster saying that Jesus was a New Age guru, an Egyptian freemason, or a hippie revolutionary. Every year or two some scholar or group of scholars comes up with a new book, full of imposing footnotes, to tell us that Jesus was a peasant Cynic, a wandering wordsmith, or the preacher of liberal values born out of due time. Some in the church are eager to jump on any new bandwagon that's going. Some, however, react by reaching for equally misleading stereotypes. A defense of a would-be supernat-

---

1. This paper is based on, and occasionally quotes from, my book *Jesus and the Victory of God* (Minneapolis: Fortress, 1996), to which reference should be made for supporting details.

4

ural Jesus can easily degenerate into a portrayal of Jesus as a first-century version of Superman — not realising that the Superman myth is itself an ultimately dualistic corruption of the Christian story. Many devout Christians content themselves with an effortless superiority: we know the truth, these silly liberals have got it all wrong, and we've got nothing new to learn. Sometimes people like me are wheeled out to demonstrate, supposedly, the truth of traditional Christianity, with the implied corollary that we can now stop asking these unpleasant historical questions and get on with something else, perhaps something more profitable, instead.

As you may expect, I do not intend to encourage any of these attitudes. As I said, I regard the continuing historical quest for Jesus as a necessary part of ongoing Christian discipleship. I doubt very much if, in the present age, we shall ever get to the point where we know all there is to know, and understand all there is to understand, about Jesus himself — who he was, what he said and did, and what he meant by it all. But since orthodox Christianity has always held firm to the basic belief that by looking at Jesus himself we discover who God is — indeed, that we discover the meaning of the word "god" itself — it seems to me indisputable that we should expect always to be continuing in the quest for Jesus, precisely as part of, indeed perhaps as the sharp edge of, our exploration into God himself.

This, of course, carries certain corollaries. If it is true, as I believe it is, that Christian faith cannot pre-empt the historical questions about Jesus, it is also true that historical study cannot be carried out in a vacuum. We have been taught by the Enlightenment to suppose that history and faith are antithetical, so that to appeal to the one is to appeal away from the other. As a result, historians have regularly been suspect in the community of faith, just as believers have always been suspect in the community of secular historiography. When Christianity is truest to itself, however, it denies precisely this dichotomy — uncomfortable though this may be for those of us who try to live in, and to speak from and to, both communities simultaneously. Actually, I believe this discomfort is itself one aspect of a contemporary Christian vocation: as our world goes through the deep pain of the death-throes of the Enlightenment, the Christian is not called to stand apart from this pain, but to share it. That is the spirit in which I offer these reflections. I am neither a secular historian who happens to believe in Jesus, nor a Christian who happens to indulge a fancy for history, but someone who believes that being a Christian necessarily entails doing business with history, and that history done for all it's worth will challenge spurious versions of Christianity, including many versions considered orthodox, but sustain and regenerate a deep and true orthodoxy, surprising and challenging though this will always remain.

2. The Necessity of the Quest

I am a first-century historian, not a Reformation or eighteenth-century specialist. Nevertheless, from what little I know of the last five hundred years of European and American history, I believe that we can categorise the challenge of the Enlightenment to historic Christianity in terms of its asking a necessary question in a misleading fashion. The divide in contemporary Christianity between liberals and conservatives has tended to be between those who, because they saw the necessity of asking the historical question, assumed that it had to be asked in the Enlightenment's fashion, and those on the other hand who, because they saw the misleadingness of the Enlightenment's way of proceeding, assumed that its historical questions were unnecessary. Let me speak first of the necessity of the Enlightenment's question, and then of the misleading way it has been addressed.

The protest of the Reformation against the medieval church was not least a protest in favour of a historical and eschatological reading of Christianity against a timeless system. Getting at the literal meaning of the texts, as the Reformers insisted we must, meant historical reading: the question of what Jesus or Paul really meant, as opposed to what the much later church said they meant, became dramatically important. This supported the Reformers' eschatological emphasis: the cross was a once-for-all achievement, never to be repeated, as they thought their Catholic opponents thought they were doing in the Mass. But, arguably, the Reformers never allowed this basic insight to drive them beyond a halfway house when it came to Jesus himself. The Gospels were still treated as the repositories of true doctrine and ethics. Insofar as they were history, they were the history of the moment when the timeless truth of God was grounded in space and time, when the action that achieved timeless atonement just happened to take place. This, I know, is a gross oversimplification, like almost everything I shall say in this paper, but I believe it is borne out by the sequel. Post-Reformation theology grasped the insights of the Reformers as a new set of timeless truths, and used them to set up new systems of dogma, ethics, and church order in which, once again, vested interests were served and fresh thought was stifled.

The Enlightenment was, among many other things, a protest against a system which, since it was itself based on a protest, could not see that it was itself in need of further reform. (The extent to which the Enlightenment was a secularised version of the Reformation is a fascinating question, one for brave Ph.D. candidates to undertake, rather than the subject for an after-dinner address about Jesus. But we have to do business with these possibilities if we are to grasp where we have come from, and hence where we may be being called to go to.) In particular, the Enlightenment, in the person of Herman Samuel Reimarus, challenged unthinking would-be Christian dogma about the eternal Son of God and his establishment of this oppressive system called Christianity. Reimarus challenged it in the name of history, the weapon that the Reformers had used against Roman Catholicism. Go back to the beginning, he said, and you will discover that Christianity is based on a mistake. Jesus was, after all, another in a long line of failed Jewish revolutionaries; Christianity was the invention of the first disciples.

I believe that Reimarus's question was necessary. Necessary to shake European Christianity out of its semi-Deistic dogmatism, and to face a new challenge: to grow in understanding who Jesus actually was and what he actually accomplished. Necessary to challenge bland dogma with a living reality; necessary to challenge idolatrous distortions of who Jesus actually was, and hence who God actually was and is, with a fresh grasp of truth. The fact that Reimarus gave his own question an historically unsustainable answer does not mean he did not ask the right question. Who was Jesus, and what did he accomplish?

This necessity has been underlined in our own century, as Ernst Käsemann saw all too clearly. Look what happens, he said, when the church abandons the quest for Jesus. In Germany, for example, the non-questing years between the wars created a vacuum in which nonhistorical Jesuses were offered in an attempt to legitimate the Nazi ideology. I would go so far as to suggest that whenever the church forgets its call to engage in the task of understanding more and more fully who Jesus actually was, idolatry and ideology lie close at hand. To renounce the quest because you don't like what the historians have so far come up with is not a solution.

But the Enlightenment's raising of the question of Jesus was done in a radically misleading manner. The Enlightenment, notoriously, insisted on splitting apart history and faith, facts and values, religion and politics, nature and supernature, in a way whose consequences are written into the history of the last two hundred years — one of the consequences being, indeed, that each of those categories now carries with it, in the minds of millions around the world, an implicit opposition to its twin, so that we are left with the great difficulty of even conceiving of a world in which they belong to one another as part of a single indivisible whole. Again, so much debate between liberals and conservatives has taken place down this fault line, while the real battle — to rearticulate a reintegrated worldview — has not even been attempted. But there is a deeper problem with the Enlightenment than its radically split worldview. The real problem is that it offered a rival eschatology to the Christian one. This needs a little explanation.

Christianity began with the thoroughly Jewish belief that world history was focused on a single geographical place and a single moment in time. The Jews assumed that their country, and their capital city, was the place in question, and that the time, though they didn't know quite when it would be, would be soon. The living God would defeat evil once and for all, and create a new world of peace and justice. The early Christians believed that this had in principle happened in and through Jesus of Nazareth; as we shall see, they believed this (a) because Jesus himself had believed it and (b) because he had been vindicated by God after his execution. This is what early Christian eschatology was all about: not the expectation of the literal end of the space-time universe, but the sense that world history was reaching, or indeed had reached, its single intended climax.

This was grasped in principle by the Reformers. Luther, I grant, saw a recapitulation of the history of Israel in the history of the church, envisaging the medieval period on the analogy of the Babylonian captivity. But his strong Christological focus prevented this from becoming a new rival eschatology, divorced from its first-century roots.

With the Enlightenment this further step was taken. All that had gone before was a form of captivity, of darkness; now, at last, light and freedom had dawned. World history was finally brought to its climax, its real new beginning, not in Jerusalem, but in Western Europe and America. Not in the first century, but in the eighteenth. It is wryly amusing to observe the way in which post-Enlightenment thinkers to this day heap scorn upon the apparently ridiculous idea that world history reached its climax in Jerusalem two thousand years ago, while themselves holding a view we already know to be at least equally ridiculous. Thus, as long as the necessary question of the Enlightenment (the question of the historical Jesus) was addressed within the Enlightenment's own terms, it was inevitable not only that Christology would collapse into warring camps of naturalist and supernaturalist, that Jesus-pictures would be produced in which the central character was either an unexceptional first-century Jew or an inhuman and improbable superman-figure, but also that liberal and conservative alike would find it hugely difficult to reconceive the first-century Jewish eschatological world within which alone the truly historical Jesus belongs. Jesus was almost bound to appear as the teacher, and perhaps at most the embodiment, of either liberal timeless truths or conservative timeless truths. The thought that he might have been the turning point of history was, to many on both sides of the divide, almost literally unthinkable. Even Schweitzer, who of course brought the eschatological perspective back with a bang, radically misunderstood it.

I believe, then, that within the multiple tasks to which God is calling the church in our own generation there remains the necessary task of addressing the Enlightenment's question, Who precisely was Jesus and what precisely did he accomplish? And I believe that there are ways of addressing this question which do not fall into the trap of merely rearranging the Enlightenment's own categories. We have a new opportunity in our generation to move forward in our thinking, our praying, our whole Christian living, no doubt by many means, but not least by addressing the historical Jesus–question in fresh and creative ways. That is the task I now wish to address.

3. New Opportunities in the Quest

Journalists often ask me why there is anything new to say about Jesus. The answer, actually, is that there both is and isn't. Mere novelty is almost bound to be wrong: if you try to say that Jesus didn't announce the kingdom of God, or that he was in fact a twentieth-century thinker born out of time, you will rightly be rejected. But what did Jesus mean by the kingdom of God? That, and a thousand other cognate questions, are far harder than often supposed, and the place to go to find new light is the history of Jesus' own times. And that means first-century Judaism, in all its complexity, and with all the ambiguities of our attempts to reconstruct it.

And, of course, there are all sorts of new tools available to help us to do this. We have the Dead Sea Scrolls, for example, all of them at last in the public domain. We have good new editions of dozens of previously hard-to-find Jewish texts, and a burgeoning secondary literature about them. We have all kinds of archaeological finds, however complex they may be to interpret. Of course there is always the danger both of oversimplification and overcomplication. Our sources do not enable us to draw a complete sociological map of Galilee and Judaea in Jesus' day. But we know enough to be able to say quite a lot, for instance, about the agenda of the Pharisees; quite a lot, too, about what sort of aspirations came to be enshrined in what we call apocalyptic literature, and why; quite a lot, too, about Roman agendas in Palestine and the agendas of the chief priests and of the Herodian dynasty in their insecure struggles for a compromised power. Quite a lot, in other words, about the necessary contexts for understanding Jesus.

We can perhaps say something, too, about Galilean peasants. Not, I think, all that some current writers would like us to say. There are those who see the peasant culture of ancient Mediterranean society as the dominant influence in the Galilee of Jesus' day, with the Jewish apocalyptic colouring decidedly muted; so that Jesus' announcement of the kingdom has less to do with Jewish aspirations and more to do with social protest. Let me stress *both* that this is a mistake *and* that showing it to be so does not lessen the element of social protest which is still to be found within the much wider-ranging and more theologically grounded kingdom-announcement which we can properly attribute to Jesus. Equally, I emphasise that one of the things we can know about peasant societies like that of Jesus is that they were heavily dependent on oral traditions, not least traditions of instant storytelling. When we get this right, we avoid at a stroke some of the extraordinary reductionism that has characterised the Jesus Seminar, with its attempt to rule out the authenticity of most Jesus-stories on the grounds that people would only have remembered isolated sayings.[2] But my overall point is simply this: there is a great deal of history writing still waiting to be attempted and accomplished, and we have more tools to do it with than most of us can keep up with. If we really believe, in any sense, in the incarnation of the Word, we are bound to take seriously the flesh which the Word became. And, since that flesh was first-century Jewish flesh, we should rejoice in any and every advance in our understanding of first-century Judaism, and seek to apply those insights to our reading of the Gospels.

We should do this not in order to undermine what the Gospels are saying, or to replace their stories with quite different ones of our own, but to understand what they are really all about as they are. It is a standard objection to historical-Jesus research to say that God has given us the Gospels and that we cannot and should not put a construction of our own in their place. This misunderstands the nature of the historical task. Precisely because these texts have been read and preached as Holy Scripture for two thousand years, all kinds of misunderstandings have crept in, which have then been enshrined in church tradition. Let me give you an obvious example. When Martin Luther rightly reacted against the medieval translation of *metanoeite* as *paenitentiam agere* and insisted upon the repentance of the heart, he could not, perhaps, see that his reading would be used in turn to support an individualistic and pietistic reading of Jesus' command to repent, which does no justice at all to the meaning of the word in the first century. Jesus was summoning his hearers to give up their whole way of life, their national and social agendas, and to trust him for a different agenda, a different set of goals. This included, of course, a

2. For a full critique of the Jesus Seminar's flagship product, *The Five Gospels*, ed. Robert W. Funk and Roy W. Hoover (New York: Macmillan, 1993), see N. T. Wright, "Five Gospels but No Gospel," in *Crisis in Christology*, ed. W. R. Farmer (Livonia, Mich.: Dove Booksellers), pp. 115-57.

change of heart, but went far beyond it. This illustrates a point which could be repeated dozens of times. Historical research, as I have tried to show in my writings, by no means tells us to throw away the Gospels and substitute a quite different story of our own. It does, however, warn us that our familiar readings of those gospel stories may well have to submit to serious challenges and questionings, and that we may end up reading even our favourite texts in ways we had never imagined. Since this agenda is thus truly Protestant, truly Catholic, truly evangelical, and truly liberal, not to mention potentially charismatic as well, I am sure that an Episcopal audience will not fail to recognise it as its own true vocation. It takes a certain courage, of course, to be prepared to read familiar texts in new ways. Let me assure you that it is abundantly worth it, and that what you lose in terms of your regular exegesis will be more than made up for in what you will gain.

4. False Trails in the Quest

In order to understand where we are in the bewildering options in today's quest, it helps to see the state of play a hundred years ago. Three figures stand out. William Wrede argued for consistent scepticism: we can't know very much about Jesus — he certainly didn't think of himself as the Messiah or the Son of God, and the Gospels are basically theological fiction. Albert Schweitzer argued for consistent eschatology: Jesus shared the first-century apocalyptic expectation of the end of all things, and, though he died without it having come about, he started the eschatological movement that became Christianity. What is more, the synoptic Gospels more or less got him right. Over against both these positions, Martin Kähler argued that the quest for a purely historical Jesus was based on a mistake, since the real figure at the heart of Christianity was the preached and believed Christ of the church's faith, not some figment of the historian's imagination.

All three positions are alive and well as we come to the end of the twentieth century. The Jesus Seminar and several writers of a similar stamp stand in the line of Wrede. Sanders, Meyer, Harvey, and several others, myself included, stand in the line of Schweitzer. Luke Timothy

Johnson is our contemporary Kähler, calling down a plague on all the houses. Since I have been criticised, sometimes quite sharply, for offering this sort of analysis, I want to say a word or two of explanation and perhaps even justification.

Schweitzer's construction of Jesus, as is well known, was so un-welcome to the theological establishment that there followed half a century of little serious Jesus-research. The so-called "New Quest" of the 1950s and 1960s made some progress at getting things started again, but never really managed to recover a serious historical nerve. Books and articles spent more time arguing about criteria for authen-ticity than offering major hypotheses about Jesus himself. By the mid-1970s there was a sense of stalemate. It was then that quite a new style of Jesus-historiography began to emerge, explicitly distinguishing itself from the so-called "New Quest." For my money, the best book of that period was Ben Meyer's *The Aims of Jesus,* which received less notice than it should have precisely because it broke the normal mould — and perhaps because it made heavy demands on a New Testament scholarly world unused to thinking through its presuppositions and methods with high philosophical rigour. Six years after Meyer, Ed Sanders's *Jesus and Judaism* continued the trend. Both books reject the New Quest's methods; both offer reconstructions of Jesus that make thorough and sustained use of Jewish apocalyptic eschatology; both offer full-blown hypotheses that make a fair amount of sense within first-century Judaism, rather than the bits-and-pieces reconstruction, based on a small collection of supposedly authentic but isolated say-ings, characteristic of the "New Quest."

In this light, I believed in the early 1980s that we were witnessing what I called a "third quest" for Jesus. This was simply a way of saying that what Meyer and Sanders and several others were doing was significantly different, in several ways that can be laid out unambigu-ously and reasonably noncontroversially, from the "Old Quest" of the pre-Schweitzer days and from the "New Quest." In this light, when the Jesus Seminar, then Crossan, and then particularly Funk himself, explicitly continued the work of the New Quest, in Funk's case making quite a point of doing so, I believe I am justified in continuing to distinguish these movements in this way. Of course, contemporary history refuses to stand still and be cut up into neat pieces. Several writers cross over the boundaries this way and that. But I persist both in maintaining the distinction between the Wrede-route and the Schweitzer-route, and in arguing that the latter offers the best hope for serious historical reconstruction.

I have argued in detail against the Jesus Seminar, and Crossan in particular, in various places, and it would be tedious to repeat such arguments in a context such as the present one. But I want to make it clear that if I disagree with Crossan, Funk, and the Jesus Seminar, and in different ways with Marcus Borg, as I do, it is not because I think they are wrong to raise the questions they do, but because I believe their presuppositions, methods, arguments, and conclusions can be successfully controverted on good historical grounds, not by appealing to theological *a prioris*. It is not enough (nor would it be true) to dismiss such writers as a bunch of disaffected liberals or unbelievers. We must engage in actual argument about actual issues.

One of the best arguments, however, is the offering of an alternative hypothesis that actually does the job a successful hypothesis must: make sense of the data, do so with an essential simplicity, and shed light on other areas. This, I believe, is what can be accomplished by some such construct as I have offered in my recent writings. Obviously there isn't time to do more than summarize a few points, and in moving now to the new opportunities in the Quest, I choose three central features that I think show most clearly how the Third Quest can stimulate and reinvigorate our view both of Jesus and, ultimately, of God. I want to speak about the kingdom of God, the meaning of the cross, and the question of the Incarnation.

5. New Opportunities in the Quest

a. Kingdom of God and Eschatology

The starting point for serious Jesus-reconstruction is to grasp more clearly than we have before the fully Jewish and fully eschatological meaning of Jesus' announcement of the kingdom of God. As I have argued at length elsewhere, the Jews of Jesus' day for the most part believed that the exile, the punishment for Israel's sins, was not yet over. If it were, the Romans would not be ruling Palestine; nor for that matter would Herod or Caiaphas. To this extent, Reimarus was quite right. The context of Jesus' proclamation of the kingdom of God was the Jewish hope for liberation.

The apocalyptic announcement of the kingdom of God, when we place it in its first-century Jewish context, was not, then, about the end of the world. It was about the great actions within history, whereby the one true and living God would act within Israel's history, and so within world history as a whole, to bring Israel's long and chequered story to its appointed climax, to liberate her from oppression, and to deal once and for all with the evil that had oppressed her. When we meet kingdom announcers in the pages of Josephus, we are not in the presence of end-of-the-world dreamers, but of political revolutionaries, people who today with our confusing categories we would call right-wing extremists. They believed, quite simply, that there was "no king but God"; and they translated this directly into action, first into a tax revolt and then into armed rebellion. These people, whom we often think of as "zealots" (though Josephus doesn't use that term until later), included the hard-line Pharisees as well as the Shammaites who would stop at nothing to bring about the purification of Israel both from Gentile oppression and from renegades within the ranks.

Political aims and goals, and the means thought fit to attain them, were no doubt every bit as complex in the Middle East in the first century as they are today. But this strand of expectation constantly recurs, in text after text and movement after movement. Three features, which are enormously important for understanding Jesus, emerge as central to the apocalyptically expressed kingdom dreams of first-century Palestinian Jews. These three features are drawn together in several prophetic passages, not least the well-known kingdom passage in Isaiah 52:7-12.

First, they hoped that the real return from exile would happen at last. Second, as the necessary corollary of this, they hoped that evil would be defeated once and for all — and by "evil" they meant not only pagans, not only compromised Jews, but the dark power that they conceived to stand behind all earthly manifestations of evil. Third, they hoped for the return of Israel's God himself, in person. What form this return would take is quite unclear. Some may have supposed that when YHWH appeared it would be, once more, like the pillar of cloud and fire in the wilderness. The great coming event would be, after all, a new exodus. And central to the whole expectation was of course the Temple. YHWH would return to the Temple. He would defeat the nations that were oppressing Jerusalem. He would liberate his people, so that they could build the Temple properly and worship and serve him in peace and freedom.

Notice carefully what follows. The expectation of the Kingdom of God was not a matter of abstract ideas or timeless truths. It was not about a new sort of religion or a new moral code. It was not a general statement about how one might go to heaven after death. It was a matter of a story that was reaching its critical moment; a history that was moving towards a climax. When Jesus announced to his contemporaries that "the kingdom of God is at hand," he was telling them that the new chapter had opened in the story they were all familiar with.

Reimarus, then, was right to locate Jesus on the map of first-century Jewish kingdom expectations. But what Reimarus and his followers to this day never grasped was that Jesus, in announcing the kingdom, consistently and radically redefined it. The kingdom was indeed breaking in; but it wasn't what people had in mind. Rather than the sort of revolution that the Maccabees had engaged in so successfully two centuries before, Jesus looked back to the prophetic paradigms, not least those in Isaiah, and made all three of the kingdom themes central to his own work, both in action and in teaching. Where he was — where he healed, feasted, and forgave, where he challenged existing slaveries — the renewed, reconstituted Israel was being formed. Where he was, the powers of evil were being defeated in ways that implied more than a mere temporary setback. Where he was, though I think this remained at most implicit until near the very end, YHWH was present, reconstituting his people, establishing his sovereignty in symbolic actions, bringing about the long-awaited ful-filment of prophecy, the climax of Israel's long and tortuous story.

In all of this — which we have no time to study in depth or detail here — Jesus was not so much like a wandering preacher preaching sermons or a wandering philosopher offering maxims, as like a poli-tician gathering support for a new and highly risky movement. But we should not imagine that politics here could be split off from theology. Jesus was doing what he was doing in the belief that in this way Israel's god was indeed becoming king. Everything pointed to the basic announcement: the kingdom of God was present, but it was not what Jesus' contemporaries had imagined.

This strange announcement is focused in certain key sayings: "The kingdom of God is at hand"; "the kingdom of God has come upon you." Scholars have debated endlessly whether Jesus thought of the kingdom as present or future from the point of view of his ministry. This discussion has recently been hijacked into the discussion of whether he spoke of an apocalyptic (future) kingdom or a nonapocalyptic kingdom (the supposed "present kingdom" of Cynic or wisdom or gnostic teaching, which I have argued is a figment of the scholarly imagination). Once we learn to think in true first-century Jewish kingdom-categories, however, there is no problem, not even a logical oddity, in embracing both present and future elements within a single apocalyptic scheme.

Consider the case of Simeon ben-Kosiba, hailed by Rabbi Akiba as bar-Kochba, the son of the star. Bar-Kochba announced the revolution against Rome in A.D. 132. He declared a new Jewish state, and minted coins carrying the new date: the year 1. If anyone had asked one of his followers whether the kingdom of God had indeed arrived at that point, the answer would be, Yes of course! To say "no" would have been utterly disloyal to the great leader, to the new movement. But if anyone were then to ask, Is there then nothing to work for, to fight for? Is the kingdom completely and purely present? the answer would again be obvious: of course there is still a battle to fight! Precisely because the kingdom is present, has truly been inaugurated, we are now committed to fighting the battle; and we shall win it. In first-century Jewish categories, then, it is no problem to think of the kingdom as present and future. It is actually a problem to think of it in any other way within the ministry of Jesus.

What, then, was Jesus' aim and intention? Where was his kingdom announcement leading? What was he going to do next? That is the question we must glance at in a moment. But before we leave the topic of the kingdom, please note. If we begin at this point in our understanding of Jesus' announcement of the kingdom, all sorts of features of the canonical Gospels come up into three dimensions and make striking historical sense. Jesus' welcome to outcasts, his healing of the sick, and his celebratory meals with all and sundry were not mere examples of a general principle — for instance, the love of God for sinners. They were the reality of which such generalisations are pale abstractions. This was what the climax of history would look like. And, please note, if this was the climax of Israel's history, the whole point of the story was that it was also the climax of the world's history. Israel's covenant God was the creator of the world; therefore, when he finally did for Israel what he was going to do for Israel, the world as a whole would be brought within the reach of his saving justice and sovereignty. If we can recapture the historical particularity of Jesus' announcement of the kingdom, rather than leave it vague or gener- alized, or suppose it to be a cipher either for the hope of postmortem heaven or the church itself, I believe we have a clear road into an evangelism and mission that will bring back together what the Enlight- enment so successfully split apart: the personal challenge of God to every man, woman, and child, and the social and political challenge of the kingdom of God to all the world.

b. The Meaning of the Cross

The historical argument for Jesus' kingdom announcement forces us toward another key question. What did Jesus think would happen next? More specifically, did he think it was part of his vocation that he should die a violent death, and if so, how did he construe that death, that vocation? This is perhaps the deepest and strangest of all the questions about Jesus, and in *Jesus and the Victory of God* it took me the longest of my chapters to get to the bottom of it. Let me simply summarize a much longer argument.

I shall assume, what I have argued fully elsewhere, that Jesus believed he was Israel's Messiah. That word does not, of course, denote a divine incarnate being. It denotes, rather, Israel's anointed king, the one in whose fate Israel's own fate reaches its climax. So it was with Jesus. In his great symbolic act of entering Jerusalem on a donkey and cleansing the Temple, he declared, for those who had eyes to see, that he was staking a messianic claim, albeit a strange one in view of post-Maccabaean expectations of a warrior king whose cleansing of the Temple would accompany the military overthrow of the gentile oppressors.

The strangeness of Jesus' claim is then focused on his other great symbolic action, the Last Supper. Carrying all the overtones of Passover, in other words, of freedom from slavery and exile, of covenantal redemption, this meal was transformed by Jesus so that it pointed not simply back to the Exodus but on to his own approaching death. He interpreted this action with a range of cryptic sayings, designed to evoke several other complementary Jewish traditions: the so-called "messianic woes"; the suffering righteous one; the martyrs; and above all the whole context of Isaiah 40–55, not least, but not exclusively, the figure of the Servant. In drawing these themes together into an unprecedented new configuration, and in applying them to himself, Jesus was announcing, again for those with ears to hear, a belief we can summarize in five sequential points, and which I suggest makes perfect sense historically:

a. that God's purposes for Israel, and hence for the world, would be effected by means of Israel's history reaching a strange but decisive moment of fulfilment and climax;
b. that this moment would consist in a time of intense suffering, through which Israel and the world would pass to God's new age;
c. that this suffering would not only be the dark path through which redemption would come, but would actually be the means by which it would be effected, by which the stranglehold of evil on Israel and the world would be defeated;
d. that this intense suffering would itself be focused on one individual;
e. that this individual would be himself, Israel's anointed representative.

Jesus' intention vis-à-vis the cross is thus correlated closely and exactly with his kingdom announcement. His death would be the final means by which his kingdom announcement would be validated. This would be the defeat of evil that would explain and undergird his implementing of the return from exile, the call of the renewed Israel. This would be the means by which God would judge and save his people Israel, and so would in principle accomplish his purposes for the whole world.

This baldest of summaries of a long and intricate argument may at least alert us to a further point at which the serious historical quest for Jesus can be of enormous value in the church's growth to maturity in our own day. Discussions of atonement theology regularly get stuck between those who think that on the cross God put into effect an abstract system of punishing evil vicariously and those who think the cross is simply an example of the wonderful lengths to which divine love will go, an act that changes people's hearts by calling forth the response of grateful answering love. I suggest that even those who consider themselves biblical theologians have ignored the historically grounded starting point of atonement theology in the self-understanding of Jesus himself: that he would go to the cross, to take upon himself the literal and historical judgment that he had predicted for the nation of Israel, to do (in other words) for Israel and the world what Israel and the world could not do for themselves. This way of approaching the cross offers, I believe, the starting point for an atonement theology which is both rich and satisfying in itself, true to all the major historic strands of subsequent thinking about the cross, and which points beyond itself, beyond the realm of ideas, to the practical vocation of those who claim to follow Jesus the Messiah: that we should be the people in and through whom is lived out and worked out the vocation, as Paul put it, to bear in our bodies the dying of Jesus, so that his life may also become manifest.

c. Jesus and the God of Israel

We come at last to the great central issue. How did Jesus conceive of his relation to the one he called Abba, Father? Here, again, there are false trails to be shunned, and, I suggest, a historically grounded way forward towards a restatement, and more than a restatement, of what we have come to call the Incarnation.

The clue to it all, I believe, has once more been overlooked by would-be orthodox theologians eager for prooftexts and not interested in the *realia* of first-century Judaism. At the heart of the Jewish kingdom expectation lay the passionate hope that YHWH himself would at long last return to Zion. I am not aware that this line of thought has been explored anywhere in contemporary writing about Jesus (apart, of course, from my own). Let me attempt to persuade you that it should be.

Post-enlightenment Christology has of course polarized, with many variations and nuances, between those who see Jesus as basically God incarnate, and then are tempted to treat that incarnation docetically, and those who see Jesus as basically the supreme human being, revealing God perhaps but not exactly *being* God. The problem is that in neither case do people regularly stop and ask what they mean by the word "god" itself. I suggest that it is far better, as a matter of method, to start at the other end. What did Jesus do and say that helps us see how he thought of himself and God?

My proposal, though large, is quite simple. We have seen that Jesus' actions in the Temple and the upper room functioned as symbols, explained by various riddles, whereby Jesus announced both his messianic vocation and his intention of bearing Israel's fate on her behalf. I suggest that these two, taken together and placed within their larger context, constitute a single, though complex, further symbolic action. Jesus' journey to Jerusalem, climaxing in his actions in the Temple and the upper room, and undertaken in full recognition of the likely consequences, was intended to function like Ezekiel lying on his side or Jeremiah smashing his pot. The prophet's action *embodied* the reality. Jesus went to Jerusalem in order to embody the third and last element of the coming of the kingdom. He was not content merely to announce that YHWH was returning to Zion. He intended to enact, symbolize, personify, and embody that climactic event.

Jesus went to Jerusalem to act out, dramatically and symbolically, YHWH's judgment on his rebel people, and his strange salvation of them from the fate he had announced. Unlike the Essenes, he was not content to wage a war of words against the Jerusalem hierarchy from a safe distance. He saw the present regime in dual focus: in terms of a servant who had buried the master's money, and in terms of rebel subjects refusing their rightful king. The only appropriate response was judgment. His parables of a returning king or master were not, then, about his second coming. They were designed to explain Jesus' actions: *he saw his journey to Jerusalem as the symbol and embodiment of YHWH's return to Zion.* But who would abide the day of his coming?

Within Jesus' prophetic and messianic vocation, we can trace the outlines of a deeper vocation that would remain hidden, like so much else, until the very end. He called the twelve into existence; he was not himself *primus inter pares.* He invoked the image of the shepherd:

a royal symbol, of course, but one that also spoke of YHWH himself as the shepherd of his people. Jesus used this image to explain what he was about, to interpret his characteristic actions and words. He spoke and acted as if he were the new lawgiver; as if he were the embodiment of the divine Wisdom. And, above all, he behaved as if he had the right to do and be what normally the Temple was and did: to be the place where and the means by which fellowship between God and Israel was restored.

How then did Jesus think of himself? He was aware, I suggest, of a vocation to do and be for Israel and the world what, according to Scripture, only Israel's god can do and be. He wasn't, in the normal sense, "aware of being God" in the way one knows one is male or female, or hungry or thirsty. He had what we may call a faith-awareness of vocation. He believed himself called, by Israel's god, to *evoke* the traditions that promised YHWH's return to Zion, and the somewhat more nebulous but still important traditions that spoke of a human figure sharing the divine throne; to *enact* those traditions in his own journey to Jerusalem, his messianic act in the Temple, and his death at the hands of the pagans (in the hope of subsequent vindication); and thereby to *embody* YHWH's return. As part of his human vocation, grasped in faith, sustained in prayer, tested in confrontation, agonized over in further prayer and doubt, and implemented in action, he believed he had to do and be, for Israel and the world, that which according to Scripture only YHWH himself could do and be. He was Israel's Messiah; but there would, in the end, be "no king but God."

I suggest, in short, that the return of YHWH to Zion, and the Temple theology which it brings into focus, are the deepest keys and clues to gospel Christology. Forget the pseudo-orthodox attempts to make Jesus of Nazareth conscious of being the second person of the Trinity; forget the arid reductionism that is the mirror-image of that unthinking, would-be orthodoxy. Focus, instead, on a young Jewish prophet telling a story about YHWH returning to Zion as judge and redeemer, and then embodying it by riding into the city in tears, symbolizing the Temple's destruction and celebrating the final exodus. He would be the pillar of cloud and fire for the people of the new exodus. He would embody in himself the returning and redeeming action of Israel's covenant God.

I hope you can see the outline of the picture that is beginning to emerge. We still, in our culture, live with the shadow of the old Deist view of God: a high-and-dry God, a God who is so transcendent that we find it difficult to think of him acting in the world at all, let alone acting with deep compassion and self-giving love. If we are orthodox Christians, living within that worldview, we struggle to say that, well, Jesus is the Lord of Glory, but somehow despite all that he came to live and to die for us. What I am suggesting is that the view of God in this traditional Western picture is quite wrong. When we address the question, Is Jesus God? Is Jesus divine? we all too often start with the Deist picture of God, and then try to fit Jesus into it. As a result, we end up with a docetic Jesus-figure, who simply strolls around being God all over the place in a way that leaves no room for vocation, for choice, for obedience, above all for Gethsemane and the cry of abandonment on the cross. Instead, the whole New Testament invites us — no, urges us, insists of us — to start with Jesus and rethink our view of God around him. And when we do that, then of course what we find is the Old Testament picture of YHWH with a human face. This is the God who says, "I have heard my people's cry, and I have come, myself, to save them." This is the God who says, "Behold, I have graven you on the palms of my hands." This is the God who, like the father in the parable of the Prodigal Son, says, "You would rather I were dead? Very well, here you are"; and who we then find running down the road, throwing his dignity to the winds, to welcome us, his prodigal children. The God who would not show his face to Moses has shown it to us on the cross. The face is wounded with the wounds of the world's pain and grief, scarred with the marks of the world's sin. It is the face that says: this have I done for my true love. On the cross, the living God says in action what Jesus said at his last great symbolic supper: this is my body, given for you.

Conclusion

Three remarks by way of conclusion. I have tried to show that when we study Jesus as a figure within first-century history we emerge with a better grounding for our Christian faith than we do if we ignore history in case it threaten that faith. But of course everything depends on the Resurrection. If this Jesus didn't rise again, then his sense of vocation is proved to be an utter self-deception. I am in the process of developing a historical argument about the Resurrection elsewhere; the Quest for the historical Jesus has not usually taken very much notice of this question, so I have deliberately excluded it from our discussion here. But it is only because of the Resurrection that we have any reason to suppose that what Jesus thought he was to accomplish on the cross has any validity at all. It is because of the Resurrection, as Paul says, that he is marked out as Son of God in power. Frankly, if Jesus of Nazareth did not rise from the dead on the third day, in a transformed but still physical body, leaving an empty tomb behind him, I as a historian simply could not explain why the early church began, and why it took the shape it did. Here as elsewhere, the study of first-century Judaism is invaluable. Since all the early Christians were Jews, we must ask, Why would a bunch of Jews who had invested messianic hopes in this particular figure, say after his shameful death that he really was the Messiah?

Second, more briefly. I have argued that the historical quest for Jesus is necessary for the health of the church. I grieve that in the church both in England and in America there seem to be so few, in a church otherwise so well educated in so many spheres, with more educational resources and helps than ever before, who are prepared to give the time and attention to these questions that they deserve. I long for the day when seminarians will again take delight in the detailed and fascinated study of the first century. If that century was not the moment when history reached its great climax, the church is simply wasting its time.

Thirdly and finally. All our historical study must be done in and for the church in its mission to the world. This is not to say that we are not open to following the argument wherever it goes, not open to reading all texts, both canonical and noncanonical. On the contrary. It is because we believe we are called to be the people of God for the world that we must take the full historical task with full and utter seriousness. Study all the evidence; think through all the arguments. There is, as I hinted at the start, a long and noble tradition of Anglican theologians doing just that. It has ever been part of our tradition that we are prepared to think through our traditions afresh. I urge you to make this part of the tradition live more fully in our own day. But as we do so we must remind ourselves again and again — as our own liturgy does in so many ways — that when we are telling the story of Jesus we are doing so as part of the community that is called to model this story to the world. The more I take part in the quest for Jesus, the more I feel challenged both as an individual and as a churchman. This is not because what I find undermines traditional orthodoxy, but precisely because the rich, full-blooded orthodoxy I find bubbling up from the pages of history poses challenges to me personally, and to all the congregations I know — challenges that are extremely demanding precisely because they are gospel challenges, kingdom challenges. At this point, being a Quester is simply the same thing as being a disciple. It means taking up the cross and following wherever Jesus leads. And the good and the bad news is that only when we do that will we show that we have truly understood the history. Only when we do that will people take our arguments, whether historical or theological, seriously. Only when we do that will we be the means whereby the Quest, begun so ambiguously as part of the Enlightenment programme, will have performed the strange purpose that I believe, under God, it came into being to accomplish. Don't be afraid of the Quest. It may be part of the means whereby the church in our own day will be granted a new vision, not just of Jesus, but of God.

Jesus: The Only Way?
Anglicanism and Religious Pluralism

ALISTER E. McGRATH

RELIGIOUS PLURALISM IS as much a fact of life today as it was in the context in which Paul first preached the gospel in Europe. It is, however, an issue of substantially greater importance today, on account of a strongly rights-oriented Western culture, especially in the United States, linked with a political polity that does not wish to disadvantage anyone on account of his or her religious beliefs. It is important to appreciate that a cultural issue is often linked in with this debate: to defend Christianity is seen to belittle non-Christian religions, which is unacceptable in a multicultural society.

Especially to those of liberal political convictions, the multicultural agenda demands that religions should not be permitted to make truth-claims, to avoid triumphalism or imperialism. Indeed, there seems to be a widespread perception that a rejection of religious pluralism entails intolerance or unacceptable claims to exclusivity. In effect, the liberal political agenda dictates that all religions should be treated on an equal footing. It is, however, a small step from this essentially *political* judgment concerning toleration to the *theological* declaration that all religions are the same. But is there any reason for progressing from the entirely laudable and acceptable demand that we should respect religions other than our own, to the more radical demand that we regard them all as the same, or as equally valid manifestations of some eternal dimension of life, or as equally valid routes to a common salvation?

My task in this essay is to explore a cluster of issues focusing on the theme of religious pluralism, especially as it pertains to the issue of salvation. It is a vast field, which becomes more and more important as Western society becomes increasingly multicultural, and as Christianity continues its expansion into hitherto non-Christian cultures, especially in the Pacific Rim. To do my theme justice, it will be necessary to consider some major themes relating to religious pluralism itself, before moving on to explore the more specific issue of salvation as an issue in this broad cluster of significant issues.

However, I wish to stress one point before going further. I believe the Anglican tradition offers us invaluable resources as we seek to deal with this issue. Anglicanism offers us the vision of a great Christian tradition, grounded in history and firmly committed to the defense and positive articulation of the great insights of the gospel — among which are the uniqueness of Jesus Christ and the gospel he has entrusted to his church. Our identity as a Christian church is dependent upon maintaining our faithfulness to Jesus Christ and to that gospel, as well as to the great tradition of faithful men and women down the centuries to whom we owe our continuing commitment as we seek to articulate and defend the gospel. Jesus Christ is not one we are at liberty to choose or change; he is the one who chooses us and demands that we change in faithful obedience to him. If we lose sight of that truth, we have lost any right to call ourselves "Christian," "Anglican," or even a "church." These are not terms we are at liberty to redefine as we please. To accept them is to accept the truths they subsume. Our central concern in this paper is with the great theme of the uniqueness of Jesus Christ as Savior and Lord.

The rise of an ideology of religious pluralism — probably best seen as a subcategory of intellectual and cultural pluralism in its own right — can be directly related to the collapse of the Enlightenment idea of universal knowledge, rather than any difficulties within Christianity itself. Often, there is a crude attempt to divert attention from the collapse of the Enlightenment vision by implying that religious pluralism represents a new and unanswerable challenge to Christianity itself. The Princeton philosopher Diogenes Allen rightly dismisses this as a spurious claim:

> Many have been driven to relativism by the collapse of the Enlightenment's confidence in the power of reason to provide foundations

for our truth-claims and to achieve finality in our search for truth in the various disciplines. Much of the distress concerning pluralism and relativism which is voiced today springs from a crisis in the secular mentality of modern Western culture, not from a crisis in Christianity itself.[1]

Yet these relativistic assumptions have become deeply ingrained within secular society, often with the assumption that they are to the detriment of Christian faith.

Commenting on the theme of "the gospel in a pluralist society," Lesslie Newbigin remarks:

> It has become a commonplace to say that we live in a pluralist society — not merely a society which is in fact plural in the variety of cultures, religions and lifestyles which it embraces, but pluralist in the sense that this plurality is celebrated as things to be approved and cherished.[2]

Newbigin here makes a distinction between pluralism as a fact of life and pluralism as an ideology — that is, the belief that pluralism is to be encouraged and desired, and that normative claims to truth are to be censured as imperialist and divisive.

The Christian proclamation has, of course, always taken place in a pluralist world, in competition with rival religious and intellectual convictions. The gospel emerged within the matrix of Judaism, and its influence expanded in a Hellenistic milieu. The rise of pluralism poses no fundamental objection to the theory or practice of Christian evangelism; indeed, if anything, it brings us closer to the world of the New Testament itself. Commenting on the situation confronted by the early church, as described in the Acts of the Apostles, the leading Anglican evangelist Michael Green remarks:

> I find it ironic that people object to the proclamation of the Christian gospel these days because so many other faiths jostle on the doorstep of our global village. What's new? The variety of faiths in antiquity

1. Diogenes Allen, *Christian Belief in a Postmodern World* (Louisville: Westminster/John Knox, 1989), p. 9.

2. Lesslie Newbigin, *The Gospel in a Pluralist Society* (Grand Rapids: Eerdmans, 1989), p. 1.

was even greater than it is today. And the early Christians, making as they did ultimate claims for Jesus, met the problem of other faiths head-on from the very outset. Their approach was interesting. . . . They did not denounce other faiths. They simply proclaimed Jesus with all the power and persuasiveness at their disposal.[3]

The early Christian expansion continued within a religiously pluralist context, as can be seen from the growth of the church in pagan Rome, the establishment of the Mar Thoma church in southern India, or the uneasy coexistence of Christianity and Islam during the period of the Islamic Caliphate. All of these are examples of situations in which Christian apologists and theologians, not to mention ordinary Christian believers, have been aware that there are religious alternatives to Christianity on offer.[4]

It is quite possible that this insight may have been lost to English or American writers of the late nineteenth or early twentieth centuries. For such writers, pluralism may have meant little more than a variety of forms of Protestantism, while "different religions" would probably have been understood to refer simply to the age-old tension between Protestantism and Roman Catholicism. Pluralism was situated and contained within a Christian context. But immigration from the Indian subcontinent has changed things in England, with Hinduism and Islam becoming foci of identity for ethnic minorities, just as France has been shaken by the new presence of Islam through emigration from its former North African colonies. As a result, Western theologians (who still seem to dominate global discussion of such issues) have at long last become aware of and begun to address issues that are everyday facts for Christians in many parts of the world, and have been for centuries.

Yet the theological approaches to other religions developed in these Christian communities have had little or no impact on Western theology. The approaches are based on explicitly stated Western as-

---

3. Michael Green, *Acts for Today: First Century Christianity for Twentieth Century Christians* (London: Hodder & Stoughton, 1993), p. 38.

4. The literature is huge. On the Arab context, see Robert B. Betts, *Christians in the Arab East* (Atlanta: John Knox, 1989). The situation in India has been surveyed masterfully by Stephen Neill, *A History of Christianity in India,* 2 vols. (Cambridge: Cambridge University Press, 1984-85).

sumptions and passively accepted by those educated in an allegedly more advanced Western context.

A discussion of Christianity's place among world religions must be conducted, first of all, on the basis of mutual respect between Christians and non-Christians, a respect expressed in dialogue, which is an attempt by people with different beliefs to gain a better understanding of each other. But this dialogue cannot be based on the deeply patronising assumption that "everyone is saying the same thing." While dialogue implies respect, it does not presuppose agreement.

The distinctive emphasis on "dialogue" within pluralism rests on a Socratic model.[5] It assumes the participants in the dialogue are all speaking of the same substantial entity, which they happen so see from different perspectives. Dialogue thus facilitates a pooling of perspectives, leading to a cumulative perception that transcends the particularities of each, enriching and informing all participants. The approach can be likened to the old parable of blind men touching an elephant for the amusement of a king's court. Their differing descriptions, though apparently irreconcilable, can be harmonized as different perspectives on a single greater reality. Each perspective is valid; on its own, however, each is a mere fragment of the greater reality.

But how appropriate is this analogy to understanding the relation between the religions of the world? Lesslie Newbigin makes a vitally important observation that needs to be weighed carefully.

> In the famous story of the blind men and the elephant . . . the real point of the story is constantly overlooked. The story is told from the point of view of the king and his courtiers, who are not blind but can see that the blind men are unable to grasp the full reality of the elephant and are only able to get hold of part of it. The story is constantly told in order to neutralize the affirmations of the great religions, to suggest that they learn humility and recognize that none of them can have more than one aspect of the truth. But, of course,

5. On this, see Michael C. Stokes, *Plato's Socratic Conversations: Drama and Dialectic in Three Dialogues* (London: Athlone Press, 1986). For the application of the method in therapy, see Tullio Marandhao, *Therapeutic Discourse and Socratic Dialogue* (Madison: University of Wisconsin Press, 1986).

the real point of the story is exactly the opposite. If the king were also blind, there would be no story. The story is told by the king, and it is the immensely arrogant claim of one who sees the full truth, which all the world's religions are only groping after. It embodies the claim to know the full reality which relativizes all the claims of the religions.[6]

Newbigin brings out the potential arrogance of any claim to be able to see all religions from the standpoint of one who sees the *full* truth. For someone to claim that they see the big picture, while Christians and others see only part, is tantamount to imperialism, unless it can be shown to be universally available, a public knowledge open to general scrutiny and critical evaluation.

The claim of privileged access to a comprehensive knowledge of reality is generally treated with scepticism, not least on account of its lack of empirical foundations, its resistance to verification or falsification. There is general agreement that there is no privileged position from which the "big picture" can be seen. Until and unless the "full reality which relativizes all the claims of the religion" is made publicly available and subjected to intense empirical analysis, the claim that all the religions somehow instantiate its various aspects is little more than idle speculation. Indeed, such a claim is both unverifiable and unfalsifiable.

It is perfectly possible for Christian to engage in dialogue with non-Christians, religious or otherwise, without adhering to the shallow and patronizing view that "we're all saying the same thing."[7] As Paul Griffiths and Delmas Lewis have stated, "it is both logically and practically possible for us, as Christians, to respect and revere worthy representatives of other traditions while still believing — on rational grounds — that some aspects of their world-view are simply mistaken."[8] Contrary to John Hick's more homogenizing approach, John V. Taylor remarked that dialogue is "a sustained conversation between parties who are not saying the same thing and who recognize

---

6. Lesslie Newbigin, *The Gospel in a Pluralist Society* (Grand Rapids: Eerdmans, 1989), pp. 9-10.

7. See Arnulf Camps, *Partners in Dialogue* (Maryknoll, N.Y.: Orbis, 1983), p. 30.

8. Paul Griffiths and Delmas Lewis, "On Grading Religions, Seeking Truth, and Being Nice to People: A Reply to Professor Hick," *Religious Studies* 19 (1983): 78.

and respect the differences, the contradictions, and the mutual exclusions between their various ways of thinking."[9]

Dialogue thus implies respect, not agreement, between parties — and, at best, a willingness to take the profound risk that the other person may be right, and that recognition of this fact may lead to the changing of positions. There is, for example, a real possibility that a disillusioned Muslim will find a Christian understanding of salvation more attractive and meaningful than her own, and convert to Christianity as a result. This phenomenon, which occurs regularly (and in many different directions) in the real world, must be accepted as part of any attempt to understand and come to terms with religious pluralism.

Dialogue is important, partly because it enhances our understanding of other religions, and partly because it acts as a gadfly, inviting us to reassess our understanding of our own faith, by forcing us to reexamine its various aspects in the light of its foundational sources. One of my interests concerns the development of Christian doctrine.[10] I have often noticed how significant doctrinal developments are in response to dialogue with those outside the Christian faith. I am not suggesting that this means that some Christian doctrines are a response to non-Christian pressures; rather, I am stating, as a matter of observable fact, that dialogue with non-Christians can provoke Christians into reexamining long-held views that turn out to rest on inadequate scriptural foundations.

To give an example: it was not that long ago that it was regarded as irresponsible and shocking for Christians to speak of God suffering or experiencing pain. Yet dialogue with non-Christians (especially Jewish writers who espouse what has come to be known as "protest atheism") provided a stimulus to reexamine the biblical and theological basis of the doctrine of the *apatheia* of God.[11] And this stimulus

9. John V. Taylor, "The Theological Basis of Interfaith Dialogue," in J. Hick and B. Hebblethwaite (eds.), *Christianity and Other Religions* (Philadelphia: Fortress Press, 1981), p. 212.

10. See my 1990 Bampton Lectures at Oxford University, published as Alister E. McGrath, *The Genesis of Doctrine* (Oxford/Cambridge, Mass.: Basil Blackwell, 1990).

11. See Rem B. Edwards, "The Pagan Dogma of the Absolute Unchangeableness of God," *Religious Studies* 14 (1975): 305-13; Jung Young Lee, *God Suffers for Us: A Systematic Inquiry into a Concept of Divine Passibility* (The Hague: Nijhof, 1974); A. E.

led to the rediscovery of the suffering of God, both in Scripture and the Christian tradition (as found, for example, in the writings of Martin Luther and Charles Wesley). Dialogue is a pressure forcing Christians to constantly reexamine their doctrinal formulations, with a view to ensuring that they are as faithful as possible to what they purport to represent or embody. Evangelicalism must be committed to the principle that the *ecclesia reformata* is an *ecclesia semper reformanda;* dialogue is one of the ways this process of self-examination and reformation continues. It is a bulwark against complacency and laziness, and a stimulus to return to the sources of faith, rather than resting in some currently acceptable interpretation of them.

Discussions about religious pluralism have been hindered within the church by well-meaning people locked into the "we're-all-saying-the-same-thing-really" worldview, which suppresses or evades the differences between faiths in order to construct a superficial theory that accounts for commonalities. The deliberate suppression of differences is academically unacceptable. The evasions cannot be tolerated if we wish to do justice to other religions as viewed by their own adherents, rather than the spurious reconstructions of these faiths produced by the homogenizing scholars of religion. A willingness to recognize differences removes the most basic criticism levelled against interfaith dialogue: that it does not acknowledge genuine differences.

Consider the dialogue between Jews and Christians, with which I have been personally involved. In an important recent study, for example, Jacob Neusner has argued that there has been *no* Jewish-Christian dialogue, in that the central belief of each faith — the doctrine of the Incarnation in the case of Christianity, and the divine vocation of Israel in the case of Judaism — has been evaded by those engaged in such discussions.[12] Can this be real dialogue, he asks, if there has been a failure to face up to such clear and overt differences? Why do these interfaith discussions seek to establish points of agreement, and pass over such major differences?

McGrath, *Luther's Theology of the Cross* (Oxford: Blackwell, 1985); W. McWilliams, "Divine Suffering in Contemporary Theology," *Scottish Journal of Theology* 33 (1980): 35-54; J. Moltmann, *The Crucified God* (Philadelphia: Westminster, 1974).

12. Jacob Neusner, *Telling Tales: The Urgency and Basis for Judeo-Christian Dialogue* (Louisville: Westminster/John Knox, 1993).

In part, the answer to his question is simple: the point of such dialogue is usually to establish commonalities, in order to enhance mutual understanding and respect in a highly polarized modern world, in which religious differences are of substantial political importance — a point stressed by Gilles Kepel of the Institute of Political Studies in Paris.[13] Yet this entirely praiseworthy goal has its more negative side. It can all too easily lead to the deliberate suppression of differences, in the interests of harmony. It is entirely proper that the religions of the world should be recognized as disagreeing with each other in matters of their beliefs. The Christian tradition regards God's final self-revelation as having taken place in Jesus Christ; Islam regards it as having taken place through Mohammed. Although agreed on the idea of a final revelation of God, the two religions differ on its mode of revelation and its content. Christians insist Jesus was crucified; Muslims insist he was not. Well, let's respect these differences. They remind us that Muslims aren't Christians, and vice versa. If the religious believer actually believes *something,* then disagreement is inevitable — and proper. As Richard Rorty has remarked, nobody "except the occasional cooperative freshman" really believes that "two incompatible opinions on an important topic are equally good."[14]

It is no crime to disagree with someone. It is, however, improper to suppress or evade such differences on account of an *a priori* belief that no such differences can exist. George Lindbeck has written of the liberal tendency to "homogenize" everything; my own approach is to honour and welcome genuine differences, and seek to explore their implications. There is no place for an intellectual dishonesty that refuses to acknowledge, for example, that Christians worship Jesus Christ as Lord and Savior, where Muslims regard the Qu'rán as the authoritative word of God and Mohammed as his prophet. Both religions are committed to evangelism and conversion (to use two Christian terms that have no exact parallels in Islam),[15] in the belief

13. Gilles Kepel, *La revanche de Dieu: chrétiens, juifs et musulmans à la reconquête du monde* (Paris: Seuil, 1991).

14. Richard Rorty, *The Consequences of Pragmatism* (Minneapolis: University of Minnesota Press, 1982), p. 166.

15. Islam, like Christianity, is a missionary religion, which is actively seeking to expand its influence in the west through conversion *(da'wah)* and territorial expansion

that they are correct; neither regards its differences as a threat to its distinctiveness. For Islam, Christianity is different — and wrong.

An Anglican Approach to Religions and Salvation

So what approach to other religions may we adopt, and what is the salvific place of Christianity within the world religious situation? In what follows, I shall apply some of the leading themes of the Anglican heritage to this question, most notably a willingness to take the ecumenical creeds with great seriousness as a framework for the proper interpretation of Scripture. The most helpful starting point in dealing with the question "Is Jesus the only way to salvation?" is to consider the notion of "salvation" itself. The Christian notion of "salvation" is complex and highly nuanced. In the New Testament, the controlling images include terms and concepts drawn from personal relationships, physical healing, legal transactions, and ethical transformation. Yet amid the diversity, one factor remains constant: however salvation is to be understood, it is grounded in the life, death, and resurrection of Jesus Christ.[16] Salvation is a possibility only on account of Jesus Christ. The early Christians had no hesitation in using the term "savior" to refer to Jesus Christ, despite the fact that this term was already widely used within the complex and diverse religious context in which the gospel first emerged. For the New Testament writers, Jesus was the only savior of humanity. On the basis of the evidence available to these writers, this conclusion seemed entirely proper and necessary. The evidence concerning Jesus needed to be interpreted in this direction, and was thus interpreted.

The New Testament thus affirms the *particularity* of the redemptive act of God in Jesus Christ.[17] The early Christian tradition, basing itself

---

(dâr al islâm): see Larry Poston, *Islamic Da'wah in the West: Muslim Missionary Activity and the Dynamics of Conversion to Islam* (New York: Oxford University Press, 1992).

16. See Alister E. McGrath, "Christology and Soteriology: A Response to Wolfhart Pannenberg's Critique of the Soteriological Approach to Christology," *Theologische Zeitschrift* 42 (1986): 222-36.

17. See Lesslie Newbigin, *The Finality of Christ* (Richmond, Va.: John Knox, 1969); more recently, Clark H. Pinnock, *A Wideness in God's Mercy: The Finality of Jesus Christ in a World of Religions* (Grand Rapids: Zondervan, 1992), pp. 49-80.

on the New Testament, reaffirmed this particularity. While allowing
that God's revelation went far beyond Jesus Christ (in that God made
himself known to various extents through such means as the natural
order of creation, and human conscience and civilization), the general
knowledge of God was not understood to entail universal salvation.
Much the same point is made in other ways by later writers. For
example, John Calvin stated the various styles of knowledge of God
available to humanity when he drew his celebrated distinction between
a "knowledge of God the creator" and a "knowledge of God the
redeemer."[18] The former was universally available, mediated through
nature and (in a fuller and more coherent manner) Scripture; the latter,
which alone constituted a distinctively Christian knowledge of God, was
known only through Jesus Christ, as he is revealed in Scripture. Thus
Calvin would have had no problems in allowing, for example, both Jews
and Muslims to have access to a knowledge of God as creator; the
particular and distinctive aspect of a Christian understanding of God
related to knowing him as redeemer, rather than as creator alone.

Calvin here expresses a long-standing consensus within Christian
theology that knowledge of God may be had outside the Christian
tradition. The same general principle is maintained in Lutheran dogmatics, and is often expressed in terms of the distinction between *Deus
absconditus* and *Deus revelatus*. As Carl Braaten expresses this, "Lutheran
theology typically affirms a twofold revelation of God: through the
hidden God of creation and law *(Deus absconditus)* and through the
revealed God of covenant and gospel *(Deus revelatus)*."[19] A similar
approach is associated with the Second Vatican Council.[20] In allowing
knowledge of God outside the specifically Christian community, I am
not saying anything new, remarkable, or particularly controversial; I
am merely reiterating a long-standing consensus within Christian
theology. Anglicanism has here held and defended insights that are
shared by Roman Catholic, Lutheran, and Reformed writers.

18. See Edward A. Dowey, *The Knowledge of God in Calvin's Theology* (New York:
Columbia University Press, 1952).

19. Carl E. Braaten, "Christ Is God's Final, Not the Only, Revelation," in Carl E.
Braaten, *No Other Gospel! Christianity among the World's Religions* (Minneapolis: Fortress
Press, 1992), pp. 65-82; quote at p. 68.

20. Miikka Ruokanen, *The Catholic Doctrine of Non-Christian Religions According to
the Second Vatican Council* (Leiden: Brill, 1992).

Nevertheless, some correctives must immediately be added, as follows:

1. The Christian tradition bears witness to a particular understanding of "God," and cannot be merged into the various concepts of divinity found in other religions. To allow that something may be known of God in non-Christian religions is not to say that all aspects of their understanding of God are consistent with Christianity, nor that every aspect of the Christian understanding of God is found in other religions. We are talking about "points of contact" and occasional convergences, not identity nor even fundamental consistent agreement.

2. In the Christian understanding, factual or cognitive knowledge of God is not regarded as saving in itself. As Søren Kierkegaard pointed out in his *Unscientific Postscript,* it is perfectly possible to know about the Christian understanding of God without being a Christian.[21] Knowledge of God is one thing; salvation is another. To allow that something may be known of God in non-Christian religions is not to imply that "salvation," in the Christan understanding of that term, is available through them.

3. Furthermore, the notion of "salvation" varies considerably from one religion to another. In the native religions of west Africa in particular, for example, there is often no discernible transcendent element associated with their notions of salvation. A certain laziness in dealing with English translations of the religious writings of other faiths, especially those originating in India and China, has given rise to the assumption that all religions share common ideas of "salvation." In fact, the English term "salvation" is often used to translate Sanskrit or Chinese terms with connotations and associations quite distinct from the Christian concept. These divergences are masked by the translation, which often suggests a degree of convergence that is absent in reality.

So important are these points that they will be explored in more detail.

---

21. Søren Kierkegaard, *Unscientific Postscript* (London: Oxford University Press, 1941), pp. 169-224. Cf. P. L. Holmer, "Kierkegaard and Religious Propositions," *Journal of Religion* 35 (1955): 135-46.

The Christian Understanding of "God"

There was a period when there was some sympathy for the idea that mutual understanding among the world's religions would be enhanced if Christians accepted a kind of "Copernican revolution" in which they stopped regarding Jesus Christ as of central importance, and instead began to focus their attention on God. Being God-centered would be more helpful than being Christ-centered.

In the end, an incarnational Christology — an essential element of classical Anglicanism — is a serious barrier to interreligious understanding only in the sense that the Islamic emphasis on the Qu'rán is also a barrier. Both are integral to the faiths in question. To eliminate them would be to radically alter the faiths, assisting interfaith reconciliation only to the extent that it destroyed the distinctiveness of the religions in question. This may be a hypothetical possibility in academic seminar rooms; in the real world, we must learn to live with conflicts between such defining and distinctive characteristics of faiths, rather than attempt to smooth them down. The religions are not putty to be molded by pluralist ideologues, but living realities that demand respect and honour.

It is a simple matter of fact that traditional Christian theology is strongly resistant to the homogenizing agenda of religious pluralists, not least on account of its high Christology. The suggestion that all religions are more or less talking about vaguely the same "God" finds itself in difficulty in relation to certain essentially Christian ideas — most notably, the doctrines of the Incarnation and the Trinity. For example, if God is Christ-like, as the doctrine of the divinity of Christ affirms in uncompromising terms, then the historical figure of Jesus, along with the witness to him in Scripture, becomes of foundational importance to Christianity. Such distinctive doctrines are embarrassing to those who wish to debunk what they term the "myth of Christian uniqueness," who then proceed to demand that Christianity should abandon doctrines such as the Incarnation, which imply a high profile of identification between Jesus Christ and God, in favour of various degree Christologies, which are more amenable to the reductionist programme of liberalism. In much the same way, the idea that God is in any sense disclosed or defined Christologically is set to one side, on account of its theologically momentous implications for the identity and significance of Jesus Christ — which liberal pluralism finds an embarrassment. Let us turn to consider these two points.

First, the idea of the Incarnation is rejected, often dismissively, as a myth.[22] Thus John Hick and his collaborators reject the Incarnation on various logical and commonsense counts — yet fail to deal with the question of why Christians should have developed this doctrine in the first place.[23] There is an underlying agenda to this dismissal of the Incarnation, and a central part of that agenda is the elimination of the sheer *distinctiveness* of Christianity. A sharp distinction is thus drawn between the historical person of Jesus Christ and the principles he is alleged to represent. Paul Knitter is but one of a small galaxy of pluralist writers concerned to drive a wedge between the "Jesus-event" (unique to Christianity) and the "Christ-principle" (accessible to all religious traditions, and expressed in their own distinctive, but equally valid, ways).

It is fair, and indeed necessary, to inquire concerning the pressure for such developments, for a hidden pluralist agenda appears to govern the outcome of this Christological assault — a point made in a highly perceptive critique of Hick's incarnational views from the pen of Wolfhart Pannenberg. "Hick's proposal of religious pluralism as an option of authentically Christian theology hinges on the condition of a prior demolition of the traditional doctrine of the incarnation." Hick, Pannenberg notes, assumes that this demolition has already taken place, and chides him for his excessive selectivity — not to mention his lack of familiarity with recent German theology! — in drawing such a conclusion.[24]

It is highly significant that the pluralist agenda forces its advocates to adopt heretical views of Christ in order to meet its needs. In an effort to fit Jesus into the mold of the "great religious teachers of humanity" category, the Ebionite heresy has been revived, and made

22. Perhaps most notably in J. Hick (ed.), *The Myth of God Incarnate* (London: SCM Press, 1977).

23. See Alister E. McGrath, "Resurrection and Incarnation: The Foundations of the Christian Faith," in A. Walker (ed.), *Different Gospels* (London: Hodder & Stoughton, 1988), pp. 79-96.

24. Wolfhart Pannenberg, "Religious Pluralism and Conflicting Truth Claims," in G. D'Costa (ed.), *Christian Uniqueness Reconsidered* (Maryknoll, N.Y.: Orbis, 1990), p. 100.

politically correct. Jesus is one of the religious options available among the great human teachers of religion. He is "one of the lads," to use a Yorkshire phrase.

Second, the idea that God is in some manner made known through Christ has been dismissed. Captivated by the image of a "Copernican Revolution" (probably one of the most overworked and misleading phrases in recent writings in this field), pluralists demand that Christians move away from a discussion of Christ to a discussion of God — yet fail to recognize that the "God of the Christians" (Tertullian) might be rather different from other divinities, and that the doctrine of the Trinity spells out the nature of that distinction. The loose and vague talk about "God" or "Reality" found in much pluralist writing is not a result of theological sloppiness or confusion. It is a considered response to the recognition that for Christians to talk about the Trinity is to speak about a specific God (not just "deity" in general), who has chosen to make himself known in a highly particular manner in and through Jesus Christ. It is a deliberate rejection of authentic and distinctive Christian insights into God, in order to suggest that Christianity, to rework a phrase of John Toland, is simply the republication of the religion of nature.

Yet human religious history shows that natural human ideas of the number, nature, and character of the gods are notoriously vague and muddled. The Christian emphasis is upon the need to worship, not gods in general (Israel's strictures against Canaanite religion being especially important here), but a God who has chosen to make himself known. As Robert Jenson has persuasively argued, the doctrine of the Trinity is an attempt to spell out the identity of this God, and to avoid confusion with rival claimants to this title.[25] The doctrine of the Trinity defines and defends the particularity and distinctiveness and ultimately the *uniqueness* of the "God of the Christians." The New Testament gives a further twist to this development through its language about "the God and Father of our Lord Jesus Christ," locating the identity of God in the actions and passions of Jesus Christ. To put it bluntly: for Christians, and supremely for Anglicans, God is Christologically disclosed. As a former Archbishop of Canterbury, Arthur Michael Ramsey, declared: "The importance of the confession

---

25. Robert Jenson, *The Triune Identity* (Philadelphia: Fortress, 1982), pp. 1-20.

'Jesus is Lord' is not only that Jesus is divine but that God is Christ-like."[26]

This point is of considerable importance. Most Western religious pluralists appear to work with a concept of God that is shaped by the Christian tradition, whether this is openly acknowledged or not. For example, pluralists often appeal to the notion of a gracious and loving God. Yet this is a distinctively Christian notion, ultimately grounded and substantiated in Jesus Christ. There is no such thing as a "tradition-independent notion of God." Even Kant's idea of God, allegedly purely rational in character and hence independent of culture, is actually ethnocentric. It has been deeply shaped by implicit Christian assumptions ingrained in Kant's social matrix. As Gavin D'Costa has pointed out, John Hick's concept of God, which plays such a significant role in his pluralist worldview, has been decisively shaped (whether he realizes or is prepared to admit this) by Christological considerations. "How credibly," he asks, "can Hick expound a doctrine of God's universal salvific will if he does not ground this crucial truth in the revelation of God in Christ, thereby bringing Christology back onto centerstage?"[27]

Pluralists have driven a wedge between God and Jesus Christ, as if Christians were obliged to choose between one or the other. As the pendulum swings towards a theocentric approach (on the assumption that the "god" in question is common to all religious traditions), the Christology of the religious pluralists becomes reduced to something of negligible proportions. Only the lowest possible Christology within the Christian tradition is deemed to be worthy of acceptance in the modern period (the awkward fact that this Christology had been rejected as heretical by the early church being passed over). If the pluralists have some infallible source of knowledge about the nature and purposes of God apart from Christ, then what is the point of the gospel? And what kind of God is it who can be known apart from Christ? Are we talking about "the God and Father of our Lord Jesus Christ" (1 Peter 1:3) — or of some different deity? An idea of God

26. Arthur Michael Ramsey, *God, Christ and the World* (London: SCM Press, 1969), p. 98.

27. Gavin D'Costa, *John Hick's Theology of Religions* (New York: University Press of America, 1987), p. 103.

can only be allowed to be "Christian" if it is subjected to the standard of God's self-disclosure through Jesus Christ, as is made known to us through Scripture.

What is the relevance of this point to our theme? Salvation, in the Christian understanding of the notion, involves an altered relation with God, whether this is understood personally, substantially, morally, or legally. But which God are we talking about? Old Testament writers were quite clear that "salvation," as they understood it, was not about a new relationship with any of the gods of Canaan, Philistia, or Assyria, but with the one and only covenant God of Israel, whom they knew by the distinguishing personal title of "the Lord." For Christianity, the notion of salvation explicitly includes and centers upon a relationship, inaugurated in time and consummated beyond time, with none other than the "God and Father of our Lord Jesus Christ" (1 Peter 1:3). We are thus dealing with a highly particularized notion of salvation, as will become clear later in this section.

The Place of Jesus Christ in Salvation

We have already touched upon the importance of Jesus Christ in relation to the Christian understanding of God, and the pluralist tendency that ends up, as Harvey Cox puts it, "soft-pedaling the figure of Jesus himself." For Cox, the most appropriate way for Christians to engage in meaningful interfaith dialogue is to begin by recognizing that "Jesus is, in some ways, the *most* particularistic element of Christianity."[28] Cox here makes the point that there is a need to begin from something concrete and historical, rather than some abstract symbol. And for Christians, this particularistic element is Jesus Christ. Christian theology, spirituality, and above all Christian worship, are strongly Christ-focused.

The New Testament, which endorses and legitimates this Christocentrism, does not merely regard Jesus Christ as *expressive* of a divine salvation, which may be made available in other forms. He is clearly understood to be *constitutive* of that salvation. In the Christian tradition, Jesus is viewed as more than *Rasál* ("the sent one," to use the Muslim

28. Harvey Cox, *Many Mansions* (Boston: Beacon, 1988), pp. 5, 6.

term for the prophets who culminated in Mohammed). He is seen as the one who establishes as much as the one who is sent — a prophet *and* a savior. Pluralists have a number of options here, from declaring that the New Testament is simply mistaken on this point (which precludes a serious claim to be Christian), or suggesting that the New Testament affirmations may be true for Christians, but have no binding force in this respect *extra muros ecclesiae* (outside the bounds of the church).[29] Yet the New Testament clearly regards Jesus Christ as, at least potentially, the savior of the world, not simply of Christians, thus pointing to the strongly universal character of his saving work.

The Nature of Salvation

John Hick has argued that there is a common core structure to all religions, which "are fundamentally alike in exhibiting a soteriological structure. That is to say, they are all concerned with salvation/liberation/enlightenment/fulfilment."[30] It seems fair to say, however, that these concepts of salvation are conceived in such radically different ways, established and attained in such different manners, that only if we are determined, as a matter of principle, to treat them as aspects of the same greater whole would we have the intellectual flexibility to do so. Do Christianity and Satanism really have the same understandings of salvation? My Satanist acquaintances certainly don't think so. In fact, Satanists accept that there is a God, but choose to worship his antithesis. This dualism hardly bodes well for a pluralist theory of the religions.

A more neutral observer, unconstrained by the need to insist that all religions are basically the same, might reasonably suggest that they do not merely offer different ways of achieving and conceptualizing salvation; they offer different "salvations" altogether. The Rastafarian vision of a paradise in which blacks are served by menial whites; the Homeric notion of Tartaros; the old Norse concept of Valhalla; the Buddhist vision of *nirvana;* the Christian hope of resurrection to

29. For a survey and criticism of these options, see Pinnock, *A Wideness in God's Mercy,* pp. 64-74.

30. John Hick, *The Second Christianity* (London: SCM Press, 1983), p. 86.

eternal life — all are so obviously different. How can all routes to salvation be equally "valid" when the goals to be reached in such different ways are so obviously unrelated?

As noted above, there is enormous variation among religions on the nature of salvation. Christian conceptions of salvation focus on the establishment of a relationship between God (in the Christian sense of the term) and his people, and use a variety of images to articulate its various aspects. Underlying these convergent images of salvation is the common theme of "salvation in and through Christ" — that is, salvation is possible only because of the life, death, and resurrection of Jesus Christ, and it is shaped in his likeness.

Differences between notions of salvation are also reflected in the various communal practices. Those who are attracted to the Buddhist notion of salvation (or any of its variants) will hardly want to become Christians, in that Christian theology, worship, and prayer are closely interwoven with a definite series of beliefs concerning the person and work of Jesus Christ. Christian worship reflects particular beliefs concerning the nature of both salvation and savior. Geoffrey Wainwright and others have emphasised the way in which theology and doxology are closely interconnected,[31] making it impossible to graft, for example, a Buddhist idea of salvation onto a Christian worshipping community. In a related context, Muslims continue to be at best highly skeptical, and more generally intensely critical of the defining Christian practice of worshipping Jesus Christ. (This practice is generally seen as an instance of the heresy of *ittakhadha,* by which Jesus is acknowledged to be the Son of God.)

With these points in mind, let us address the question: Is salvation possible outside Christianity? Post-Wittgensteinian theologians have become acutely sensitive to the need to establish the context in which words are used.[32] For Wittgenstein, the *Lebensform* ("form of living") to which a word referred and within which it was used was of decisive importance in establishing the word's meaning. Yet the term "salva-

31. Geoffrey Wainwright, *Doxology: The Praise of God in Worship, Doctrine and Life* (New York: Oxford University Press, 1980). For a more recent discussion, see Aidan Kavanagh, *On Liturgical Theology* (New York: Pueblo, 1984). The Latin formula *lex orandi, lex credendi* is often used to summarize this interrelationship.

32. A theme explored with considerable skill in Fergus Kerr, *Theology after Wittgenstein* (Oxford: Blackwell, 1988).

tion" is often used in a very loose and undefined manner. In Wittgenstein's view, the particularities of a way of life or "form of living" are of controlling importance to our understanding of concepts.

> Would it be correct to say that our concepts reflect our life?
> They stand in the middle of it.

The Christian *Lebensform* is thus of controlling importance in understanding what the Christian concept of salvation implies, presupposes, and expresses. As Wittgenstein himself pointed out, the same word can be used in a large number of senses. One way of dealing with this might be to invent a totally new vocabulary, in which the meaning of each word was tightly and unequivocally defined. But this is not a real option. Languages, like religions, are living entities, and cannot be forced to behave in such an artificial way. A perfectly acceptable approach, according to Wittgenstein, is to take trouble to define the particular sense in which a word should be understood, in order to avoid confusion with its many other senses. This involves a careful study of its associations and its usage in the "form of living" to which it relates.[33] "Salvation" is clearly a a case in point. Its use and associations within the Christian tradition, especially in worship, point to a distinctive understanding of what the Christian faith is understood to confer upon believers, its ultimate basis, and the manner in which this comes about.

If the term "salvation" is understood to mean "some benefit conferred upon or achieved by members of a community, whether individually or corporately," all religions offer "salvation." All — and by no means only religions — offer *something*. However, this is such a general statement that it is devoid of significant theological value: All religions, along with political theories such as Marxism and psy-

---

33. Ludwig Wittgenstein, *Lectures and Conversations on Aesthetics, Psychology and Religious Belief* (Oxford: Blackwell, 1966), p. 2: "If I had to say what is the main mistake made by philosophers . . . I would say that it is that when language is looked at, what is looked at is a form of words and not the use made of the form of words." There is an interesting parallel here with Barth's statement that the expressions which make up the "spoken matter of proclamation" in the Christian faith "acquire their meaning from the associations and contexts in which they are used" (Karl Barth, *Church Dogmatics,* 13 vols. [Edinburgh: T & T Clark, 1936-75], I/1, p. 86).

chotherapeutic schools such as Rogerian therapy — may legitimately be styled "salvific." The statement "all religions offer salvation" is thus potentially little more than a tautology. Only by using the most violent of means can all religions be said to offer the same "salvation." Respect for the integrity of the world's religions demands that "salvation" be particularized — that is, the distinctive morphology of a religion's understanding of salvation (including its basis, its mode of conveyance and appropriation, and its inherent nature) must be respected, and not coercively homogenized to suit the needs of some pressure group within the academy.

The distinctive character of each religion may and must be affirmed: Buddhism offers one style of "salvation," just as Christianity offers another. It is no criticism of Buddhism to suggest that it does not offer a specifically Christian salvation, just as it is not in the least imperialist to state that the Christian vision of salvation is not the same as the Buddhist. It is essential to respect and honor differences here, and resist the ever-present temptation to force them all into the same mold.

In the light of this approach, the following statements may be set out.

1. Christianity has a particular understanding of the nature, grounds, and means of obtaining salvation.[34] And the Christian understanding of salvation, like the Christian notion of God, is Christologically determined. Just as it is illegitimate to use the term "God" in a vague and generic sense, allowing it to be understood that all religions share this same divinity, so it is improper to use the term "salvation" as if it were common to all religions. When used within the context of a given religion, the English word "salvation" (which often translates Greek, Hebrew, Arabic, Sanskrit, and Chinese terms of considerably greater complexity than is appreciated) takes on specific overtones that prohibit it from designating the same concept in each case. "Salvation" is a particularity, not a

---

34. On the third point, the importance of the doctrine of justification by faith through grace must be noted. See Alister E. McGrath, *Iustitia Dei: A History of the Christian Doctrine of Justification,* 2 vols. (Cambridge: Cambridge University Press, 1986).

universality. There is an urgent need to pay more attention to the vocabulary and associations of "salvation" across the religions, rather than allowing verbal vagueness to generate theological confusion.

2. Christianity is the only religion to offer salvation *in the Christian sense of that term.* This verbally clumsy sentence acknowledges the point, stressed by Wittgenstein, that there is a vital need to make clear the associations of terms, and the particular senses in which they are being used. In that the word "salvation" is meaningless unless its context is identified, it is necessary to establish the "form of living" which gives the word its distinctive meaning — in this case, the Christian world of doctrine, worship, and hope, going back to the New Testament and consolidated in the Christian tradition.

3. Salvation, in the Christian sense of that term, is proclaimed as a real and attractive possibility for those who are presently outside the Christian community. The entire enterprise of evangelism, now recognized to be of such vital importance to the Christian churches throughout the world, is directed towards the proclamation of this good news to the world.

Conclusion

Greek mythology tells of a figure called Procrustes, given to lurking on the road from Megara to Athens, who had the disagreeable habit of sawing off the feet of dinner guests who were too big to fit in the bed he provided. Procrustes was disposed of by the hero Theseus; nevertheless, distinctly Procrustean habits of thought persist in the study of religions, with several prominent writers in this field being prepared to eliminate aspects (including key beliefs) of religions not easily accommodated by their reductionist approaches to the subject. Anglicans have every right to resist these trends and demands, and ask that the catholic and apostolic view of Jesus be affirmed today as essential to authentic Christianity in general, and to authentic Anglicanism in particular. I do not see that we need to abandon or radically modify our faith in the uniqueness of Jesus Christ. To affirm the uniqueness of Christ is not an act of arrogance, but of integrity.

Ignatius of Antioch once wrote: "wherever Jesus Christ is, there is also the universal church."[35] Anglicanism has the privilege of being part of that church. Perhaps it needs to be reminded that the privilege carries with it major responsibilities — not least of which is remaining faithful to the gospel entrusted to it, and on which it depends for its integrity, identity, and existence.

35. Ignatius, *To the Smyrnaeans,* 7. See J. Stevenson (ed.), *A New Eusebius* (London: SPCK, 1957), p. 48.

Jesus and His Atoning Work

FLEMING RUTLEDGE

Part One: Resistance to the Cross

A friend of mine, an editor who also happens to be a Roman Catholic, asked me about the book I am writing. Several other people were listening, so I took more of a risk than I usually do and said, "It's about the most important event in the history of the world — the Crucifixion." Everyone considered this. Then my Catholic friend said, "No, no; the most important event is the Resurrection."

It is easy to see how a statement such as mine might lead to misunderstanding. This is likewise true of St. Paul's declaration to the Corinthians, "I determined to know nothing among you except Jesus Christ *and him crucified.*" Did this mean that St. Paul thought the Resurrection to be of inferior importance? Clearly not, since his same letter to the Corinthians comes to its climax in the longest piece of sustained writing about the Resurrection that we have in all the New Testament. In the preaching of the early church, the Crucifixion and Resurrection functioned as a single event. There could have been no thought of separating them, or elevating one over the other. If you're making a ham and cheese sandwich, you don't ask which is more important, the ham or the cheese. If you don't have both of them, it isn't a ham and cheese sandwich. You can't have the Crucifixion without the Resurrection. The Resurrection is the mighty act of God to vindicate the Crucified One, to declare him the victor over sin, evil, and death. At the same time, however, the One who is risen is also the One who was crucified. It is not a coincidence that "Doubting Thomas" asks to see the marks of the nails and the spear in the Lord's body. The book of

49

Revelation is an extended hymn to Christ the Conqueror, but he is nevertheless "the Lamb standing *as if he had been slain*" (Rev. 5:6).

The reason Paul said to the Corinthians, "nothing among you except Jesus Christ and him crucified," is not that he considered Easter to be of no importance. It was because the Corinthians wanted Easter without Good Friday. This tendency is equally true of the American church. You know H. Richard Niebuhr's famous description of us in *The Kingdom of God in America:* "A God without wrath brought men without sin into a kingdom without judgment through the ministrations of a Christ without a cross." When this happens, we may have religiosity, we may have spirituality, but we do not have Christianity.

The cross is everywhere recognized as the principal symbol of Christianity, but we may rightly inquire whether we are ready to embrace its significance. There is much timidity in many of our churches about proclaiming its meaning. There is often more enthusiasm for teaching the Incarnation, the Creation, the teachings of Jesus about the kingdom of God, the creation of the new community and the inclusion of all people than there is for the cross. There is massive evidence from the New Testament, however, that the apostolic preaching of the earliest church grounded all these other aspects of the *kerygma* precisely in the event of the Crucifixion. In other words, the Creation, Incarnation, kingdom, new community, and especially the inclusion of all people are not theologically grounded unless they are set explicitly in the context of the Crucifixion. It is the cross that gives Christian theology and ethics its unique character. For this reason the climactic Christological statement in Mark's Gospel ("Surely this man was the Son of God") is placed on the lips of a Gentile at the moment of Jesus' death on the cross.

The Crucifixion is the touchstone of Christian authenticity, the unique feature by which everything else, *including the Resurrection,* is given its proper significance. The four Evangelists say the same thing indirectly by giving much more space to the Passion narratives than to anything else in the story of Jesus. When Jesus, in John's Gospel, repeatedly refers to his "hour of glory," he means not the Resurrection, but the Crucifixion. Without the cross at the center of the Christian proclamation, the Jesus story becomes just one among many stories about a charismatic spiritual figure (not to mention an Egyptian freemason).[1] It is the Crucifixion that marks out Christianity as something definitively different in the history of religion. It is in the Crucifixion that the nature of God is truly revealed. We go on, therefore, to reassert that the Resurrection is God's mighty Yes to the Crucified One, and that the Crucifixion is the most important thing that has ever happened — as indeed Dr. Wright said in his lecture.

The principal argument of this first part of my remarks is the resistance of American Christianity to the theology of the cross. Like much of the early church, we prefer gnosticism. Gnosticism is a hot ticket in American publishing. Just as gnosticism was the chief popular rival to Christianity in early New Testament times, so it is today. It is incomparably more likely that a book about gnosticism will be reviewed in a major secular publication than a book about classical Christianity. All the more noteworthy, therefore, is gnosticism's studied lack of interest in the Crucifixion. Luke Timothy Johnson, commenting on the gnostic gospels, points out that they lack narrative structure, and then continues:

> Even more strikingly, the Gnostic gospels lack passion accounts. The death of Jesus is either omitted or touched on only lightly. Their emphasis is on the revelation of the divine. In the canonical gospels [by contrast] the passion accounts play a central and decisive role. The emphasis of the canonical gospels is on the suffering of the Messiah. . . . In Gnostic Christianity, the enlightenment of the mind enables the avoidance of suffering.
>
> The canonical gospels view Jesus from the perspective of the resurrection . . . but in sharp contrast to the Gnostic gospels, which have *only* that perspective, the canonical gospels hold that vision of power in tension with the reality of Jesus' suffering and death. . . . In none of the canonical gospels is the scandal of the cross removed in favor of the divine glory. In each, the path to glory passes through real suffering.[2]

So once again we see that if the Resurrection is detached from the cross, we have a form of world-denying gnosticism, as in the Corinthian

---

1. This is a reference to a remark made by N. T. Wright in his lecture the night before.
2. Luke Timothy Johnson, *The Real Jesus*, pp. 150-51.

church, instead of the concept of redemptive suffering which is honored nowhere in the world more eloquently than in the civil rights monuments of Birmingham, Alabama.

The only word used in the Apostles' and Nicene Creeds in connection with the entire span of Jesus' life is "suffered." "Born of the Virgin Mary, suffered under Pontius Pilate, was crucified, dead and buried." What way is that to describe the life and ministry of a man so famous for his teachings, parables, healings, exorcisms, and other miracles? None of these things are even mentioned. The wording of the Creed is a vivid demonstration of the early Christians' certainty that the Passion summed up everything that Jesus was and did, so as virtually to eclipse everything else in the magnitude of its significance. Yet various versions of Christianity stripped of suffering are more common than ever in white America.

An example of a North American theologian making important contributions to the theology of the cross is the Canadian Douglas John Hall. His work has some fairly serious deficiencies, in my judgment, but they are to some extent outweighed by his emphasis on the cross as a "conquest from within" the human condition, which means from within the human experience of pain, limitation, abandonment, and despair. Speaking of the *theologia crucis,* he insists that the Christian community is known by this as by nothing else. If we are to claim our true identity, we need to renounce shallow optimism and positive thinking, especially in North America where these attitudes have deep roots. He calls for the church to understand itself as the community of the cross, the community that suffers-with, the community that willingly bears the stigma of the Passion in service to others. He declares that "the basic distinction between religion and [Christian] faith [is] the propensity of religion to avoid, precisely, suffering: to have light without darkness, vision without trust and risk, hope without an ongoing dialogue with despair — in short, Easter without Good Friday."[3]

Jürgen Moltmann is even more incisive. The theology of the cross, he writes, *"is not a single chapter in theology, but the key signature for all theology."*[4] The names traditionally associated with this *theologia crucis*

3. Douglas John Hall, *God and Human Suffering,* p. 126.
4. Jürgen Moltmann, *The Crucified God.* All Moltmann quotations are from this volume.

are those of Paul the Apostle and Martin Luther. This might be enough to cause some people to turn up their noses at it forever, these two figures being as controversial as they are. In our own time, however, it is not possible to deny or ignore the voices emerging from the underground to testify of its power. Thus Dietrich Bonhoeffer and and J. Christiaan Beker and many others who have spoken out of the subhuman depths of World War II have guided us forward to a new understanding of the cross as *crux probat omnia* ("the test that proves everything" — Luther). When Moltmann, for instance, calls for attention to Good Friday in all its "profane horror and godlessness," he speaks as one who has observed profane, horrible, and godless events and has determined not to turn away from them to a theology of escape. Theologian Kosuke Koyama has observed, "Jesus Christ is not a quick answer. If Jesus Christ is the answer, he is the answer in the way portrayed in crucifixion."[5] And once again Moltmann reminds us that "Christians who do not have the feeling that they must flee the crucified Christ have probably not yet understood him in a sufficiently radical way."

In the debate about the "historical Jesus" that dominates the media coverage of religion in the 1990s, the balance struck in the New Testament between the ministry of Jesus and his Crucifixion/Resurrection (understood as one event) is upset. The attempt to reconstruct the "real" Jesus from what is imagined to lie behind the accounts of his teaching is dependent on various reductive accounts of his death and resurrection. The ringing statements of the apostle Paul about the world-transforming significance of the cross and Resurrection ("If Christ has not been raised, your faith is futile and you are still in your sins" — 1 Cor. 15:17) are deemed by the reconstructionists to be dishonest theological accretions, having no truthful relation to the man they present, variously, as an Essene mystagogue, a Galilean *chasid* or charismatic wonder-worker, a healer and sage, a political revolutionary, a gay liberator, a peasant Cynic, or a teacher of spiritual wisdom who held out an alternative vision of life.[6] None of these interpretations of Jesus ascribes any significance whatever to his cross; his execution is assumed to be either a mistake by the authorities or

5. *Mount Fuji and Mount Sinai* (London: SCM, 1984), p. 241.
6. Summarized in Johnson, *The Real Jesus,* chapter 2.

a predictable end for one who troubles the Establishment. In contrast, the New Testament — taken as a whole — presents Jesus' Crucifixion, validated by the Resurrection, as the defining thing about him. I myself believe that *the strongest argument against the varous reconstructions based on the life of Jesus of Nazareth without reference to the significance of his cross is that if he had not been vindicated by God in the Resurrection, we would never have heard of him.*

And so to sum up this first part of my address: The cross of Christ is the touchstone of our faith. From the beginning it has caused offense, as blessed Paul makes clear in his statement to the Corinthians that the cross is "a stumbling block to the Jews and foolishness to the Gentiles." It is typical of American Christianity, as it is of American culture, to push the cross out to the margins; a more upbeat and triumphalist form of proclamation and practice is typical of us. Scripture and the creeds, by contrast, call the Christian community to a more intentional commitment to the way of suffering on behalf of others as the way of redemption. "Blessed are you when men revile you and persecute you and utter all kinds of evil against you falsely on my account. Rejoice and be glad, for your reward is great in heaven" (Matt. 5:11-12).

Part Two: The Meaning of the Cross

In his lecture Professor Wright gave us a persuasive account of Jesus' self-understanding as he went to the cross. I found it moving. I myself was trained to give pride of place to Jewish apocalyptic, as Wright does. During my twenty-two years of parish ministry, however, I discovered myself subjecting any ideas I might have picked up to a simple test: "Will it preach?" If the conclusion of Dr. Wright's address was a sample, the answer must be a resounding "Yes." I hope that what I offer will be seen as complementary to what he has given us, even though I will be coming at the subject from a more homiletical, literary, and pastoral perspective.

Many Christians of both sexes wear crosses around their necks, and indeed I do myself, but there is widespread ignorance and confusion about the meaning of the symbol. This second section of my address will be focused on the interpretation of the Crucifixion. There will unavoidably be places along the way where it will seem as though I am speaking of the Atonement as an isolated event. Please understand that throughout I assume that the Crucifixion and the Resurrection are a single phenomenon, even though I will not keep saying so.

First of all we need to divide the subject into two portions, the *concept* of atonement in the first place, and then the various *theories* of atonement. It was interesting to hear the word "atonement" used freely for the first time in a while during the Million Man March. My own impression is that the word and the concept have been seriously out of fashion for a long time, especially among the intelligentsia. For example, Rebecca West's abhorrence of the whole idea of atonement has recently come to the fore again because it is a feature of her classic work about the Balkans, *Black Lamb, Grey Falcon*. On the other hand, T. S. Eliot's *The Cocktail Party* is rarely performed, read, or studied today, but I recently heard the great English actress Eileen Atkins read a portion of it, as follows:

> The Unidentified Guest at the cocktail party turns out to be Sir Henry Harcourt-Reilly, psychiatrist (played by Alec Guinness in the original production). Celia Coplestone comes to see him. The doctor asks about her problem.

Celia: It sounds ridiculous — but the only word for it
That I can find, is a sense of sin.
Reilly: You suffer from a sense of sin, Miss Coplestone?
This is most unusual.
Celia: I don't mean sin in the usual sense . . .
I don't feel as if I was immoral . . .
I've never noticed that immorality
Was accompanied by a sense of sin . . .
My bringing up was pretty conventional —
I had always been taught to disbelieve in sin. . . .
Anything wrong, from our point of view,
Was either bad form, or was psychological. . . .
I don't see why mistakes should make one feel sinful!
And yet I can't find any other word for it.
It must be some kind of hallucination;
Yet at the same time, I'm frightened by the fear
That it is more real than anything I believed in.

Reilly: What is more real than anything you've believed in?
Celia: It's not the feeling of anything I've ever *done,*
Which I might get away from, or of anything in me
I could get rid of — but of emptiness, of failure
Towards someone, or something, outside of myself;
And I feel I must . . . *atone* — is that the word?

Eliot has caught the sense of disdain that the world today feels towards
the theological conception of sin, and at the same time is showing us
the way that a need for atonement persists in sneaking back into the
human drama. Having identified two ways in which the world and
the church react to the idea of atonement for sin, and moving along
to grapple with various interpretations of the cross, I propose that the
themes and motifs concerning the Crucifixion can be roughly grouped
in two categories (taken from a discussion by Paul Ricoeur):

1. Sin and guilt for which atonement must be made; sin as a responsible guilt which must be forgiven (the Crucifixion understood as sacrifice for sin).
2. Slavery, bondage, oppression from which we must be delivered
   or liberated; sin as an alien power which must be eradicated (the
   Crucifixion understood as the New Exodus, as Christ's victory
   over the powers of sin and death, commonly called the Christus
   Victor theme).[7]

Some people seem to think that we should make a choice to
emphasize either one or the other of these. I believe this insistence is
a grievous mistake, one which has led us into serious error, not only
theological but also ethical and practical. (And, indeed, bad theology
always leads to bad practice.) Today I urge that both these categories
are of utmost importance to the Apostles and Evangelists and therefore
to us.

The history of the church has been marked by bitter disputes
about the nature of the Atonement, with various individuals and
parties insisting that only one explanation of it is correct and others
erroneous. This has been a difficult stance to maintain, since there

7. Paul Ricoeur, *The Symbolism of Evil.*

was never a Council of Nicea or of Chalcedon to determine the orthodox position about the meaning of the cross, as there was about the nature of Christ and the Holy Trinity. During the greater part of this century there has been in the Episcopal Church a strong reaction against "theories" of the Atonement. We may be in sympathy with this position. "Theories" are spun out of human imagination, and we are dealing here with an event far beyond human imagination. In my judgment, the Crucifixion is not to be understood in terms of theories like the penal substitution theory or the ransom theory or any other unproven theory (and that is certainly what these are — unproven — for no one has been able to agree about them over a period of two millennia). The theories have produced a polarized situation in the church, with the majority of Episcopalians, theologically informed or not, ranged in the Christus Victor camp and an ardently evangelical subgroup equally if not more insistent about commitment to the substitutionary atonement as the *sine qua non* of a genuinely Christian position. To those of you whose eyes may be glazing over at this point, I recount a story told to me by the great American writer, Joseph Mitchell, who was a member of Grace Church in New York City until his death in 1997. As he sat by the deathbed of his sister, she asked him, "Buddy, what does Jesus' death on the cross a long time ago have to do with my sins now?" Joe, who was an instinctive theologian, certainly not a trained one, struggled to find the right words as you would expect a writer to do, and finally said, stammering as he often did, "S-somehow he-he was *our representative.*" All "theories" fall away in the space between that question and that answer.

Theories tend to be narrowly focused, tendentious, and restrictive. Metaphors, however, are open-ended and fluid, and that is what we have in the Old and New Testaments. In that sense, Joe Mitchell and his sister are better readers of the Bible than a hundred textual critics. The Bible gives us images — images drawn from many sources that make a kaleidoscopic, inexhaustibly rich picture from which to draw meaning and sustenance for all times and in all generations. No one image can do justice to the whole; all are part of the great drama of salvation: the Passover lamb, the sin offering, the scapegoat, the ransom, the sacrifice for reconciliation, the vicarious substitute, the victor on the field of battle, the representative man — each of these and all of these have their place, and the cross is diminished if any one is omitted. The foundation stone of my argument is the conviction that we need to understand the meaning of the Crucifixion in all its manifold aspects.

Now, having said that with the greatest possible emphasis, my intention is to argue against the current tendency in the church to disparage, dismiss, or ignore the clear statement of the New Testament that Jesus died *for our sin.* Just as there can be no complete account of the Crucifixion unless the themes of liberation are clearly identified, so there will be a reduced understanding if there is no deep personal response to the problem of sin. The news that one is a sinner is to be received with joy, for it is the beginning of the true journey home.

In order to show how the knowledge of sin is encompassed by joy and gladness, I refer to the music of Johann Sebastian Bach. Bach's unique contribution to the church's worship is the way he frequently combines dance forms, and their capacity for inspiring delight, with passages of the deepest anguish in the Passions and the cantatas. Jaroslav Pelikan, in his writing about Bach as theologian, calls this "confession and celebration." Part of the effectiveness of the music at these points is Bach's affinity for Martin Luther's "awareness of the human predicament" called *Anfechtung.*[8] This will help us to understand how Celia Coplestone's knowledge of sin, a sense of unworthiness, a feeling of estrangement, and all other manifestations of *Anfechtung,* rightly understood from within the context of saving grace, bring happiness and lightness to the heart. No great artist, writer, or composer has excelled Bach in this insight and capacity to bring it to joyous life. It is instructive to remember that in the time when Bach was composing his church music, Protestant orthodoxy (not yet one hundred years old) was hard-pressed to defend itself against the intellectual trends of the time, even though the Reformation was far more compatible with new discoveries and free thought. Bach's cantatas and Passions were written in an atmosphere of polemic against those who would reduce Christ to the status of a human teacher and his death to an unfortunate misapprehension. It was like St. Paul all over again: "The word of the cross is foolishness to the Greeks." Over

---

8. Jaroslav Pelikan, *Bach among the Theologians* (Philadelphia: Fortress, 1986), pp. 21-22.

against those who would call it foolishness, Bach ecstatically celebrates the victory won on the cross while at the same time insisting, as St. Paul does, upon its shame and degradation and therefore its profound appeal to those who suffer today.

We come before the cross by confessing our own sin and shame. In this way we align ourselves with what happened on Calvary. Confession of sin means willingness to confront pain. It is the opposite of that well-known modern phenomenon which we all love to sneer at: denial. People who are "in denial," as we say, are unable or unwilling to admit that something is wrong. In order to understand the Crucifixion, we need to admit that something is very wrong in human life and needs to be put right. The African-American church has something to teach us here. When I was at Union Seminary, there was a difference in the way that the black and white students looked at the idea of Christ's death as atonement for sin. A thousand years ago, Anselm of Canterbury taught that Jesus' death "made satisfaction" for sin.[9] This idea lies behind the phrasing of Thomas Cranmer's eucharistic prayer ("a one, perfect and sufficient sacrifice, oblation and *satisfaction* for the sins of the whole world"). Cranmer and Anselm are currently out of favor in many quarters. The black students at Union, however, were drawn to Anselm's theme. They knew what was at stake. I always think of an episode a few years ago in Teaneck, New Jersey, when a young, unarmed black boy, Philip Pannell, was shot by white police officers when his hands were raised in surrender. His anguished father cried, "Somebody has got to pay!" Similarly, Anselm wrote, "God's justice must be satisfied." If Anselm's conception is released from its scholastic matrix to become a fluid, suggestive figure of speech — rather than a rigidly schematic "theory" — then we are free to see with the eyes of faith that somehow, on the cross, *the Son of God himself is doing the paying.* It was always a mistake to get involved with literalistic interpretations of the biblical motifs. When Paul wrote to the Corinthians that they were *bought with a price,* he meant to evoke the Savior on the cross, not to encourage anyone to start speculating about who the price was to be paid to. Some of you may not be aware that, a couple of decades ago, the literal-minded among us almost succeeded

9. Anselm of Canterbury, *Cur Deus Homo?*

in expunging the third verse of "There is a green hill far away" from our hymnal:

> There was no other good enough to pay the price of sin;
> He only could unlock the gate of heaven and let us in.

Thanks be to God, there are plenty of Episcopalians with poetic imagination, and the verse was restored — though the liturgical police did succeed in having an asterisk placed beside it to suggest that it really would be best omitted.

I was at Christ Church, Grosse Pointe, preaching during Holy Week. While I was there I read something written by a member of the congregation, a prosperous and successful man by the world's standards. He wrote, "Most people have difficulty with the concept of sin." This is true. This difficulty keeps people away from the cross. The layman went on to say that being a Christian leads us into "recognizing that each of us, including myself, sins in thought, word, and deed *on a daily basis.* Busy-ness, lack of patience, failure to be thoughtful, a sharp tongue — all are evidence of our sinful nature." He writes further that we need to acknowledge that "we are all sinful creatures deserving of no special treatment before God."[10] The great words of Thomas Cranmer are applicable here; we ask God to look upon us "not weighing our merits, but pardoning our offenses." If we but knew it, there is great power in the act of repentance. When we acknowledge our solidarity with other sinners, we experience God's mercy as never before. This is the prayer Jesus commended: "God have mercy on me, a sinner" (Luke 18:13).

If this is true of individuals, how much more true is it of groups? Think of how difficult it is for any country or corporate identity, *including our own,* to admit that it has done anything wrong. We do not want to give up our superior position. I remember P. W. Botha, then the Afrikaner president of South Africa and, as such, the leading exponent of apartheid in his nation, saying "I hate no Black man. I hate no white man. I hate no colored man. But I intend to continue my way of life." P. W. Botha's determination to continue his way of life has been overturned by the power of God working through Nel-

---

10. I have recast Mr. Bruce Birgbauer's words very slightly in order to emphasize that repentance is not a *condition* of God's grace and mercy, but the *result* of it.

son Mandela and the churches of South Africa in one of the most powerfully unlikely deliverances from bondage into freedom ever seen in history. Here the imagery of the Passover and Exodus find their most recent application, as we sing during Eastertide: "God has brought his Israel into joy from sadness; loosed from Pharaoh's bitter yoke, Jacob's sons and daughters, brought them with unmoistened foot, through the Red Sea waters." It is the Christus Victor theme realized.

There is a revealing contrast right now on the international scene. In South Africa an extraordinary process is going on. Former Anglican Archbishop Desmond Tutu is head of a special commission that is conducting hearings about atrocities committed by the government and police during the apartheid era. Nelson Mandela's administration has no interest in inflicting retribution. Mandela has set a personal example by reaching out to whites and pursuing pragmatic, future-oriented policies. The decision has been made, however, that there will be no amnesty for torturers and murderers without full disclosure. Disclosure is the purpose of Bishop Tutu's hearings. I recently read that the details given by survivors of the brutalities they endured caused the famously effervescent Archbishop to put his head down on the table in the courtroom and weep. The hearings achieved their first major breakthrough a couple of months ago when a few Afrikaners finally admitted that Stephen Biko had not died of self-inflicted wounds after all, but had been beaten to death. All of this is in sharp contrast with Guatemala. The so-called Truth and Justice Commission in Guatemala has been given no charge to make anyone account for anything. No one will have to confess to anything, no one will have to face anyone in court, no one will have to name names. The families of the thousands of victims have raised their voices in anguish to no avail. There has been no "satisfaction" in Guatemala.

My purpose in mentioning these matters is to show, first, how a willingness to suffer and a commitment to truth and justice are linked to one another, and how the cross reveals to us the decisive act of God in Christ as the One who would take the suffering of the world into himself. Even more, the Crucifixion shows us how our Lord entered into the condition of those who were powerless, those who were voiceless, those who were made to disappear, those who were of no account in the world. The death of Jesus is not like the deaths or executions of other famous and/or admirable persons. It was neither premature, nor an unfortunate mistake, nor a tragic end to his mission. *The Crucifixion was itself his mission.* The proclamation of the church and the overwhelming witness of the New Testament is that the Son of God came into this world with the express purpose of giving himself up to death; moreover, the death that he chose was in no sense a heroic martyr's death, but the death of a common criminal in shameful, Godforsaken circumstances. His death does not belong on the list of martyrs' deaths. It is unique, and it has a unique significance. And so Jürgen Moltmann writes:

> From the very first, the Christian faith was distinguished from the religions which surrounded it by its worship of the crucified Christ. In Israelite understanding, someone executed in this way was rejected by his people, cursed amongst the people of God by the God of the law, and excluded from the covenant of life. "Cursed be everyone that hangs on a tree" (Galatians 3:13, Deuteronomy 21:23). Anyone who, condemned by the law as a blasphemer, suffers such a death is accursed and excluded from the circle of the living and from the fellowship of God.

Moltmann refers here to the teaching of Paul that "Christ became a curse for us" and that "God made him to be sin who knew no sin, that in him we might become the righteousness of God." Jesus did this in a way that is unimaginable for us, because none of us has ever had to give up what he had to give up in order to be the Savior of the human race. Not only did he willingly, voluntarily give up his divine prerogatives; even more important, he gave up his unbroken relationship with the Father. "My God, my God, why hast thou forsaken me?" We cannot plumb the depths of the Cry of Dereliction, but in it we hear something of what it meant for our Lord "to become sin." St. Paul's mysterious utterance ("God made him to be sin") has never been fully understood, but many commentators have noted its relationship to the Cry of Dereliction. "God made him to be sin who knew no sin," and in that indescribably terrible and unique moment Jesus apparently felt the full force of utter separation from the Father. That is what he underwent in order to "make us the righteousness of God." He became sin;

we become righteousness. As one of our greatest Holy Week hymns puts it:

> Lo, the Good Shepherd for the sheep is offered;
> The slave hath sinnèd, and the Son hath suffered;
> For our atonement, while we nothing heeded,
> God interceded.

We are the ones who should have been accursed, but Jesus took the curse upon himself, in our place, as our substitute. The entire witness of the Old Testament leads up to this. The more I study it, the more I preach it, the more I call upon it for pastoral ministry, the more it seems to me to be the heart of the meaning of the Atonement. It is not enough to call upon the pathos. Many deaths in human history have been profoundly moving. There is more to this death than that, and the Cry of Dereliction is the key. It is in the Godforsakenness of the cross of Christ that we see the gravity of sin, the true nature of the human predicament, and the astonishing and humanly unimaginable response of the love of God in his only begotten Son.

It is important to understand that we do not see in the cross a wrathful Father doing something terrible to an innocent Son. Nothing could be further from the truth of what is going on in the Garden of Gethsemane and on Calvary. What we see is that Jesus, the representative man, our substitute, not only *shows us how* human will aligns itself with God's will, but also *makes it happen,* in his own person; and then, in the greatest act of love that has ever taken place, he gives his own person to us. The death of Jesus on the cross is the Father and the Son acting together, with one will, for one purpose — to deliver you and me from the condemnation that the Son of God bore away from us.

In the scene from *The Cocktail Party,* Celia Coplestone says that she feels she herself must atone for her sinfulness. This is the final religious defense of the human being. We must do it ourselves. We must attain somehow to righteousness. Only a few days ago I was called in to try to help an elderly woman who is tormented by something she did fifty years ago. I wonder how the church has failed her all these years. I think for too long we have allowed people to believe that "God helps those who help themselves." How many of the people who are in your congregations believe that? Recently I met a woman who had been teaching Sunday School for twenty years, and she told me that "God helps those who help themselves" is the sum and substance of the Bible. Here is what the Bible actually says, in Paul's epistle to the Romans: "While we were *still helpless,* at the right time Christ died for the ungodly" and "God showed his love for us in that *while we were still sinners,* Christ died for us." What is the bottom line of the human condition? It is *our human defenselessness.* That is the lowest common denominator. That is the biblical foundation of a true inclusiveness that no trendy ideology of inclusiveness can even touch for comprehensiveness and radicality. It is therefore no coincidence that a favorite hymn at the time of death is this: "Help of the helpless, O abide with me."

Part Three: The Proclamation of the Cross

The biblical proclamation is that the shameful execution of Jesus and his Resurrection from the dead was, and is, the central event of all time. In this event, the Almighty Creator God has taken definitive and final action against the hostile powers that cripple and enslave humankind. This is a preposterous claim. How can a disgraceful death overcome sin and evil? Our faith is based on this paradox: a shameful, Godforsaken death has been the means of the conquest of sin and evil for all people and for all time.

The biblical metaphors have indescribable power when they are connected, in proclamation, to the human predicament. When Jesus, according to Paul in Galatians, *became a curse for us,* it was in some ineffable way a satisfaction for the sin and sufferings of all time. This cannot be apprehended in any way except by faith, but it is by faith that so many have overcome — precisely through suffering. Only a few days ago in Salisbury, Connecticut, where I am presently serving, I attended a class taught by a white man who had spent several weeks in and out of jail with Martin Luther King during the civil rights struggle. He reminded us that every night there were church services with preaching. It was the proclamation that sustained the struggle.

I will take my courage in my hand and say that at this point in our history the Episcopal Church is lacking in bold proclamation.[11]

11. The opposite is true here at the Cathedral Church of the Advent.

The seminaries are not emphasizing it and the parishes are not demanding it. It is as though the church has been anesthetized against the power of its own gospel. It is an alarming contrast to the apostolic preaching. The overwhelming impression given by the New Testament *kerygma* is that of a revolution in human affairs. The first epistle of Peter speaks of this new preaching as "the things which have *now* been announced to you by those who preached the good news to you . . . things into which angels long to look" (1 Pet. 1:12). The word *now* is often used in the epistles to indicate the brand-new state of being that exists as a result of Christ's cross and Resurrection. This radical newness, this transformation, is epitomized by the very frequent appearance in the letters of Paul and Peter of the phrase "But now . . ." (νυνὶ δέ). Paul uses it six times in Romans; for example, "*But now* the righteousness of God has been manifested apart from law . . . the righteousness of God through faith in Jesus Christ for all who believe" (3:21). The occurrences in 1 Peter are especially striking: "Once you were no people *but now* you are God's people; once you had not received mercy *but now* you have received mercy" (2:10) and "For you were straying like sheep, *but now* have returned to the Shepherd and Guardian of your souls" (2:25). A passage from Ephesians, couched in the sweeping language typical of that great letter, puts it this way: "Therefore remember that at one time you Gentiles in the flesh . . . were at that time separated from Christ, alienated from the commonwealth of Israel, and strangers to the covenants of promise, having no hope and without God in the world. *But now* in Christ Jesus you who once were far off have been brought near in the blood of Christ" (Eph. 2:11-13).[12]

The Crucifixion of Jesus, incomparably reversed by the Resurrection, is the *novum,* the new factor in human experience, the event that makes the New Testament proclamation unique in all the world. The claim of the early church was that the historical death of Jesus "under Pontius Pilate," followed by the metahistorical event of the

---

12. Examples of New Testament passages in which *but now* or *now* are used in this way, to indicate the turn of the ages at the cross, are Romans 3:21, 5:9-11, 6:22, 7:6, 8:1, 11:30, 13:11, 16:26; 1 Corinthians 7:29, 13:12; 2 Corinthians 5:16, 6:2; Galatians 2:20, 3:25, 4:9; Ephesians 2:13, 5:8; Colossians 1:22, 1:26, 3:8; Philemon 9, 11; 1 Peter 2:10, 2:25; Hebrews 12:26.

Resurrection, had changed everything for all time. It would be impossible to overemphasize the boldness and comprehensiveness of this claim. As modern people, we do not need to be reminded that this claim does not fit the way the world sees itself. Staking this claim in our post-Enlightenment environment requires considerable courage. The cultural elite of America are contemptuous of Christian faith. St. Paul's great asseveration, "I am not ashamed of the gospel," has more relevance now than ever. It is fashionable today to set aside the Crucifixion and Resurrection of Jesus, reconstructing him solely on the basis of his teaching and ministry. Being out of fashion is painful for most of us.

It has always been very difficult for the church to hold on to the cross as its center. The temptations to push it out to the margin have been tremendous from the beginning. The early Christians constantly had to defend themselves against the charge of irreligiousness. The cross as godless object was appalling not only to the Jewish sensibility but also to the Roman. In those early days of the church, the cross was not the sign in which one conquered, but a "sign of contradiction and scandal, which quite often brought expulsion and death."[13] How much more dangerous it was then for Christians to insist with Paul on *Jesus Christ and him crucified* than it is for us today; we are more familiar with the accusation of bad taste than we are with the threat of death on his account. For us, being *ashamed of the gospel* is likely to mean being embarrassed, but for the Apostles and those who responded to their message, the consequences of the cross could be life-threatening. The church where I am now serving has windows all around the nave of the twelve apostles. I find it deeply nourishing to look at them and think about how they gave their very lives so that I could hear the message two thousand years later and then proclaim it from the pulpit. I would join my voice to that of Dr. McGrath, who summoned us to a clearer vision of what will sustain the church. People are starving to death in our churches for lack of proclamation. Those beautiful feet on the mountain, for all too many, are just not there; what we hear instead are poorly digested religious ideas taken over from the culture and exhortations to be politically correct. It is a long way from the explosive *but now* of the gospel.

13. *Ibid.*, p. 34.

Scholars will continue to debate endlessly the relationship of Jesus' own attitude to his death with that of the early *kerygma* dynamically present in the canonical New Testament. We may be thankful for Dr. Wright's presence in, and commitment to, the debate about the historical Jesus. The average layman and parish priest out there on the front lines will have to continue to struggle with the current fashion in certain academic and ecclesiastical circles today to make much of the discrepancy between who Jesus actually may have been and who the church says he was. I am not ashamed today to speak *from faith for faith*. If it's good enough for Paul and Silas, it's good enough for me.

It is time for Christians with intellectual and scholarly interests to stop hanging our heads in embarrassment when we are challenged. Christian people do not need to worry about having the upper hand, but neither do we need to worry about those who would ridicule the faith once delivered to the saints. We have a great gospel, the greatest the world has ever known. To us as to the shepherds quaking on the hillside on Christmas Eve, as to the women stunned by the sight of the stone rolled away on Easter Day, the angel of the Lord says, "Fear not."

Jesus and Culture

WALTER V. L. EVERSLEY

THIS ESSAY OFFERS a theological response to the Jesus Seminar's new quest of the historical Jesus. The leaders of the seminar, whose principal works on Jesus I have in mind as I proceed, are Marcus Borg, John Dominic Crossan, and Robert Funk.[1] They claim to look for Jesus everywhere but inside the church. They seem bent on following in the footsteps of the parents of Jesus immediately after leaving Jerusalem when he was twelve years old. They have lost Jesus. Members of the Jesus Seminar are as welcome in the temple today as Mary and Joseph were to find Jesus in the Temple doing theology. The church has not lost Jesus; the church still knows and proclaims him. This conviction undergirds this essay.

The Jesus of the church is the Jesus of the canonical Gospels. He is the one professed in the catholic creeds as the Second Person of the Trinity who came from God the Father, rose from the dead, and lives now at the right hand of God and in the communities of the faithful. The Holy Spirit leads people to know Jesus through the variety of means I am suggesting. Jesus continues to be accessible to everyone, literate and nonliterate, by the power of the Spirit. The Jesus

---

1. Their principal books include Marcus Borg, *Jesus: A New Vision* (San Francisco: HarperCollins, 1991); *Meeting Jesus Again for the First Time* (San Francisco: Harper-Collins, 1994); John Dominic Crossan, *The Historical Jesus* (San Francisco: Harper-Collins, 1992); *Jesus: A Revolutionary Biography* (San Francisco: HarperCollins, 1995); Crossan with Richard Watts, *Who Is Jesus?* (New York: Harper Paperbacks, 1996); Robert Funk, *Honest to Jesus* (San Francisco: HarperCollins, 1996); Robert W. Funk, Roy W. Hoover, and the Jesus Seminar, *The Five Gospels* (San Francisco: HarperCollins, 1993).

Seminar speaks about a historical Jesus who can only be recognized through learning, and only by the literate.

As distinct from a historical study, my theological approach in this essay will be affective, appealing to the heart, the reason, and the senses. Jonathan Edwards provides a widely known example of affective analysis in his *Treatise Concerning the Religious Affections,* in which he explores the noetic, psychological, and spiritual depths of understanding.[2] My affective approach, which imitates Edwards', includes aesthetics. In other words, to appreciate the valencies of the truth about Jesus more adequately, we shall enter doors of music, look through windows of art, and touch the heart of Jesus through prayer.

In the five sections that follow, I will first attempt the philosophical task of examining the role of history in the new quest. This is unavoidable because history is the cornerstone of the Jesus Seminar's building. The scholars call themselves historians. Paying some attention to history will help me show why I believe hearing, seeing, and touching, the subjects of the next three sections, are essential modes in coming to know Jesus. The brief last section, the conclusion, will point to possible further developments of the ideas adumbrated here.

Obviously, I think the sources of data and the method of the new quest are far too circumscribed for our times. They reflect the late nineteenth-century manuscript-bound quest, which was dominantly ratiocinative and ignored the Holy Spirit. The twentieth century has traveled far beyond that. Nowadays, scholars also access truth and meaning through pictures and music; and if the scholars are Christian, through the meeting of the human spirit and the Holy Spirit.

Any major scholarly enterprise that largely confines itself to a cognitive medium of communication does itself and its audience a disservice. The Seminar itself has successfully popularized its existence through diverse public media, yet it presumes to speak of Jesus on the basis of the written word only. This, I believe, is a serious failing, indicative of age-old scholarly models. The Seminar professes to be a highly collaborative enterprise of more than seventy-five scholars, and I would like to imagine that at least a few of them have competencies in art and music.[3]

---

2. *The Works of Jonathan Edwards,* 2 (New Haven: Yale University Press, 1969).
3. Source: Funk, *The Five Gospels,* pp. 533-37.

The Seminar's attempt to make Jesus into a bandit and a revolutionary turns out to be almost banal, compared with its decision-making process — casting their votes in red, pink, gray, and black beads.[4] This has captured the public imagination; ordinary people can picture themselves playing this probability bead game. It also suggests the power of the non-verbal approaches I'm hoping to explore here.

History Revisited

Years ago, when I was a graduate student in philosophical theology, Paul Tillich's sermons excited me. So before I enrolled in a seminar on his *Systematic Theology,* I read his essays and brief treatises. Although his architectonic and fascinating use of language impressed me, I found it increasingly difficult to consent to his many terms and conclusions, particularly his Being and New Being, synonyms for God and Jesus. They struck me as contrived and irreligious. But I didn't know how to articulate my objections, so I turned to my teacher, Gordon Kaufman, for help.

Gordon Kaufman taught me a rule that pertains to this essay. He said that persuading people to our point of view lies in getting them to accept our vocabulary, our premises, and the parameters we give a problem. Only to the extent that they reply in our terms would we consider their answers truly responsive. Kaufman explained that influential scholars often capitalized on an old vocabulary by nuancing familiar terms in different ways. In other words, people felt compelled to respond to Tillich in terms of his ontology; to Bultmann in the vocabulary of myth.

Members of the Jesus Seminar have taken a similar route in their search for Jesus. I reject this route. It needs radical renovation. The members of the Seminar insist that the true Jesus becomes known through historical methods of their devising and on the basis of documents of their own choosing. They honor David Friedrich Strauss and other pioneers of the First Quest of the historical Jesus, all of whom failed in their quest. Fully aware that the eschatology of Schweitzer's *The Quest of the Historical Jesus* sounded the death knell

---

4. Borg, *Meeting Jesus Again,* p. 21. *The Five Gospels* is printed in the four colors.

for the First Quest, the Jesus Seminar rejects eschatology. It seeks instead an existential Jesus.

But the existential is a category of multiple meanings. To help themselves, Marcus Borg attempts to shift the difficulties of existentialism by drawing attention to the ambiguities of eschatology.[5] But putting existentialism into a vague historical context makes it more imprecise, especially when trying to construct a Jesus who lives only in the past. Studying that Jesus is an indulgence in antiquarianism. He has no institutional home. He lives only in the minds and writings of Seminar participants. Here I would want to agree with them — *their* Jesus has no future. His life has no true doxological meaning and no salvific purpose, the two indispensable criteria for estimating the current and continuing value of the Jesus of the church.

All historically significant persons live in three dimensions of time. They have a stable persona rooted in a past, preserved and transmitted to us in rituals and teaching by a living community faithful to the existence and memory of the personage. They have a present in the community of the faithful and a future of one kind or another. Without a future, they die. We can scarcely expect the church to disregard all we know already about Jesus to construct an entirely new persona in the light of a few manuscripts recently taken seriously by scholars who profess little allegiance to the church.

The integrity of his persona by no means precludes changes in our understanding of who Jesus is. Besides, the church has a duty to help persons meet the Jesus who befriends us in the cross, cares for us today, and walks with us into our unknown future. Scholars for whom the church is the primary location of service treat history differently from those who regard the academy as their principal spiritual home and the prime beneficiary of their scholarship. The church knows a Jesus who understood the meaning of his life and his future on the basis of his Father's kingdom, which he proclaimed as a present reality in our hearts, in history, in the future. He taught his disciples to pray for it in the Lord's Prayer. He insisted that the Holy Spirit enabled us to understand his relationship with his Father, which defined his own existence (John 14–16). The Spirit guarantees the future of the kingdom.

5. Marcus Borg, *Jesus in Contemporary Scholarship,* (Valley Forge: Trinity Press, 1995), pp. 70-74; *Meeting Jesus Again,* pp. 29, 103.

Jesus considered empowerment by the Holy Spirit, not history, the mandate for his ministry. He proclaimed this in the synagogue at Nazareth where he quoted from Isaiah, "The Spirit of the Lord is upon me because he has anointed me to preach glad tidings" (Luke 4:16-30). His hearers clearly understood his application of the text to himself, and they were sufficiently offended to want to kill him.

More than once in his ministry, Jesus pointed to his works "by the finger of God," as validation of his Messiahship. When the disciples of John asked, "Are you the one who is to come or shall we wait for another?" Jesus instructed them to tell John of the miracles he performed and the good news he preached to the poor, then declared, "Blessed is anyone who takes no offense in me" (Matt. 11:2-5). Jesus spoke in a similar vein when the Pharisees accused him of working miracles through the power of the devil. He insisted that he did so by the power of the Holy Spirit (Luke 11:20-22). Jesus also enjoined his followers to wait for the fullness of the Spirit for empowerment to implement the missionary mandate he had given them to preach the kingdom (Acts 1:8). This Spirit and the kingdom of God give Jesus historical identity and meaning throughout the Scriptures and in the church.

The continuous teaching of the church makes the doctrine of the Trinity the content of theology and the context of the life of Jesus. His integrity comes from sharing the life of God in the Trinity. He remains "yesterday, and today, and forever the same" (Heb. 13:8). In his major work *Concerning the Trinity,* St. Augustine analogizes the intratrinitarian relations to love relations. The Father represents love, the Son the object of that love, and the Holy Spirit the reciprocity of love of Father and Son.[6] Jesus is identifiable as a historical person through the church, but his identity transcends historical categories. The Jesus of the church has an established past, a viable present, and a certain future that unfolds as it comes to us, to follow the usage of Wolfhart Pannenberg, and in God's eternal future unknown to us.[7]

---

6. For a recent, thorough, and brief discussion of the love of God and the unity of the Trinity in the mold of Augustine, see Wolfhart Pannenberg, *Systematic Theology,* trans. G. Bromiley (Grand Rapids: Eerdmans, 1991), 1:422-448.

7. Trans. Geoffrey W. Bromiley, *Systematic Theology* (Grand Rapids: Eerdmans, 1991), 1:54-55.

We enter into the love relationship with God through the Son by the power of the Holy Spirit and thereby learn to love others. Without the Trinity and the divine economy in creation, Christian morality loses its theological foundation. Thus we cannot agree with the Jesus Seminar that Jesus is merely a moral teacher. His relationship with God gives Christian morality a uniqueness that differs from philosophical ethics.[8] A historical Jesus who is independent of the Trinity lacks the divine authority to order our religious and moral life.

To justify their Jesus, the Jesus Seminar has created a fifth gospel on which it chooses to rely to extend the range of material in its search for the historical Jesus. This inclusion in the Jesus Seminar's canon stops the Seminar from saying what is a genuinely responsive answer to their work. No ecumenical council or Christian denomination has ever canonized Funk's fifth gospel. Contrary to the Seminar's arbitrary action, the church sees the Bible as a sacred text with which we ought to avoid tinkering, for it discloses the Word of God to us by the Spirit.

The Seminar's search for the authentic words of Jesus in *The Five Gospels* suggests an honorable scholarly task. But it also reflects an undesirable biblical fundamentalism. Most Christians have relied on a broader tradition, not an alleged verbatim reportage of the words of Jesus as the basis of Christian doctrine. Most of us read and interpret the Bible with a strong sense of literary, allegorical, and spiritually applicable meanings. Respondents to the Seminar may properly rely on data time-honored by the church and the wider community of scholars as a basis for its portrait of Jesus. Hence, an appeal to canonical Scripture, catholic creeds, ancient and historic hymns, validated both within and without the Christian community, has more ostensible legitimacy for speaking about Jesus than documents privately perused by a privileged coterie of scholars.

The Jesus Seminar makes history a self-authenticating category. For them, hoary time bestows sacredness and moral value to documents that acquire probative value equal to sacred Scripture merely by age. This is unacceptable. History cannot authenticate itself. The values, judgments, and interpretations of historians usually provide

---

8. James Gustafson discusses the ethical ramifications that arise from serious consideration of the status of a Jesus who is Creator and Redeemer in *Christ and the Moral Life* (New York: Harper & Row, 1968).

the criteria for authentication. We should also be wary of making too large a claim for history as a definitively validating category for 2,000-year-old documents, as if their authors intended to write history. History itself is a discipline of comparatively recent vintage.

If, for the sake of discussion, we are willing to be silent about this for a moment, we will still have to mention that historical coherence has never been a persuasive enough criterion to undermine truth and religious belief. Richard R. Niebuhr explains through learned analysis that historical denigration of the Resurrection is an example of historical overreaching. He demonstrates the inability of historical reasoning to undermine the viability of the doctrine of resurrection by arguing that if truth depends only on what has been true in the past then we can never know new truths.[9]

Christians also insist on God's prerogative to act inconsistently vis-à-vis our expectations. They regard Jesus' resurrection as his greatest miracle.[10] In any search for Jesus, the Resurrection's impact on the life of his followers should persuade us to take it seriously, particularly in the context of a historical conversation about him. Jürgen Moltmann shares and extends this opinion by arguing that Christian thinking about Christ today needs to consider history from the perspective of the Resurrection, and the Resurrection from the perspective of history and nature.[11]

Jesus Seminar scholars consider the resurrection irrelevant. Their historical Jesus is the pre-Easter Jesus.[12] Their separation of the pre-Easter and the post-Easter Jesus bifurcates Jesus. The denigration of the Resurrection betrays a theological agenda, and requires a theological response. Christians are Easter people who have always regarded the pre-Easter Jesus and the post-Easter Jesus as one and the same person. Without the resurrection, Christian faith is vain (1 Cor. 15:14).

Marcus Borg's *On Meeting Jesus Again for the First Time* makes

---

9. *Resurrection and Historical Reason* (New York: Charles Scribner's Sons, 1957).

10. John Polkinghorne makes a similar point from a physicist's point of view. See *Serious Talk: Science and Religion in Dialogue* (Valley Forge: Trinity Press, 1995), pp. 14-15.

11. Jürgen Moltmann, *Jesus Christ for Today's World,* trans. Margaret Kohl (Minneapolis: Augsburg Fortress, 1994), pp. 71-87.

12. Borg, *Jesus in Contemporary Scholarship,* p. 171.

another disjunction. He speaks of the historical Jesus and the Christ of faith, an obsolete distinction. He accepts the first but rejects the second. But the Chalcedonian confession of two natures in one person continues to represent a merged perspective from which we see the one Lord Jesus Christ: the glory of God among us who teaches us to worship God aright; who also became "incarnate for us and for our salvation." This dynamic Jesus offers salvation from sin in this world and the hope of heaven in the hereafter. Faith in him magnetizes our moral compass. Thus we find in Jesus more than the mere moralist of the Seminar.

Its religious subject matter notwithstanding, the Seminar's program remains humanistic. Its history is an inert romantic philosophical construct too secular for believers. No Spirit is at work in this world. Like Descartes in his *Discourse on Method,* the Seminar renounces everything that isn't congenial to its faith-emptied mind. Even Hegel, by no means a champion of the Third Person of the Trinity, would reject such a method. In his *Phenomenology of Spirit* he insists that a spirit (*Geist*) is at work in the world, transforming history.[13]

The Jesus Seminar's static view of history requires us to return to a Jesus who has to be disinterred from ancient manuscripts. I much prefer Hegel's understanding of history as a mighty swelling river, alive and growing in size the further it is pushed from its source. Each generation maintains the original heritage by improving it within a normative tradition of interpretation. The church has long ago acted on this conviction. The Jesus of the church becomes known through the activity of the Holy Spirit both within and without the community of the committed. In this way, God himself prepares the world for our evangelism efforts. History is more than a philosophical construct, it is an ecclesiological category. The church lives to worship God and minister to others in specific times and places.

My respectful treatment of history in the preceding paragraphs presumes that it is an appropriate category for theological discussion. But a few reservations are in order. I agree with Luke Timothy John-

---

13. George Hegel, *The Philosophy of History,* trans. J. Sibree (New York: Dover Publications, 1956), p. 17. Hegel's *The Phenomenology of Mind,* trans. J. B. Baillie (New York: Harper Torchbooks, 1967), is a history of immanent spirit. See George Litchtheim's Introduction, pp. xxii-xxxi, for a helpful clarification of this.

son, who excoriates the Jesus Seminar for its cavalier exploitation of the term by interchanging popular and scholarly meanings.[14] Historical knowing is limited, contingent on interpretation and imagination.

In talking about history, we need to include the perspectives of those raised, as I was, in the third world. Such people tend to see history as a suspect category. It is usually written by the conquerors. Conversation about any Jesus of history makes me wonder whether this is the history of the conquered or the conquerors. Data other than written sources help us to avoid decisive dependence on a history that raises as many questions as it answers.

Robert Funk claims that only scholars have a right to lead the search for the historical Jesus. Surely literacy cannot be a prerequisite to knowing Jesus. If the Jesus of the Seminar's awareness is worth knowing, his portrait should appeal to the learned and the illiterate, the old and the young.

Oral and visual traditions in the prayers, the music, and the art about Jesus bridge the distances between the literate and the non-literate. Icons, statuary, sacraments, and sounds have a large place in the church. These are of inestimable value to worshippers irrespective of their education. Attention to this repository of data about Jesus demands a wider range of skills and scholarship than the Seminar demonstrates. Unfortunately, the Seminar continues to tread the beaten path of the language and categories of our German predecessors in the age before TV, PC, Fax, and the Internet. Technology must change scholarship for us to maintain credibility and intelligibility in the dominantly sight-and-sound world we now occupy.

Our deeply imbedded faith in literacy has gone very far towards making the knowledge of a few languages a mark of superior preparedness for understanding the gospel narratives about Jesus. As a result, many seminary graduates have a patina of learning in Greek or Hebrew, which testifies more to tolerance of academic imposition on innocents than improvement on their ignorance of the Gospels and Scripture. The Jesus Seminar treasures the tradition that honors the reading of Scripture in our own language (or preferably a dead one), hoping that it will yield the truth about Jesus. This optimistic yet

14. *The Real Jesus: The Misguided Quest for the Historical Jesus* (San Francisco: HarperCollins, 1997), pp. 81-104.

unproven proposition maintains a gulf between the literate and the illiterate, a gulf wider than the deep ditch Lessing encountered when he discovered the necessity of faith for believing in God.

We expect reading to result in more than acquaintance with ideas on a page. Reading invites believing. John writes his Gospel hoping to help his readers to believe in Jesus as the Messiah (John 20:31). By contrast, Robert Funk claims to write to find out what he believes.[15] He modifies this solipsistic claim by expressing a desire to appeal to six varieties of disgruntled persons. However, the desire to know and the ability to read can be limited means for forming faith or finding truth. Philip's encounter with the Ethiopian eunuch in the desert reminds us of this. The Ethiopian reads but fails to grasp the truth about Jesus (Acts 8:26-39).

Although I'm reluctant to recommend deconstruction, we may still gain insight from the writings of Jacques Derrida, Mark Taylor, and others. They caution us against too high a dependency on documents, which by their very nature convey simultaneously a diversity of legitimate meanings. The deconstructionist warning implies a need to extricate ourselves from the ruts that biblical and theological scholarship have followed for too many decades.

Hearing Jesus

When I noticed the assigned subject of my contribution, "Jesus and Culture," I rejoiced. The title resonates with that of H. Richard Niebuhr's classic, *Christ and Culture*.[16] In principle, Niebuhr has made my task easier by placing the discussion of Jesus within the broadest possible framework, a context accessible to all. We all share and contribute to culture in one way or another. Niebuhr defines culture in terms of universals that are still applicable today. He considers it as social, human achievement, a world of values, a conservation of values,

15. Robert Funk, *Honest to Jesus*, p. 11.
16. H. Richard Niebuhr, *Christ and Culture* (New York: Harper Torchbooks, 1951). The recently issued *Theology, History, and Culture* (New Haven: Yale University Press, 1996), from his unpublished writings, reinforces and expands what Niebuhr had already made public.

or the temporal and material realization of values, attainable by effort.[17] This means, ideally, that culture inculcates virtue and vice versa. When we place Jesus at the center of our values, culture transcends itself and conduces to sanctification.

Niebuhr's definitions are ample enough to include music. Music liberates us to travel to ethereal realms. Karl Barth notes that its performance requires a discipline that gives joy. He recognizes its power to communicate with the spirit.[18] Hans Küng's *Mozart: Traces of Transcendence* makes plain his awareness of the power of music to transcend categories.[19] These theologians discover music as a means of helping us to notice such features of Jesus as his voice. The voice of Jesus receives attention in the New Testament. Lazarus heard his voice. His sheep continue to hear it. Jonathan Edwards spoke of his voice as one of his excellencies.[20] The Gospels and the experience of the saints shape how we hear the voice of Jesus, which encourages us to listen with natural ears and the ears of the heart. I mention the voice of Jesus as an issue that can bear further development. His voice and the wordless sounds of music bridge wide distances between literate and nonliterate persons.

Music without words, such as Felix Mendelssohn's fascinating set, "Songs without Words," captures the spirit. When Jaroslav Pelikan places Bach among the theologians he does so because of Bach's perspicuous use of biblical texts in the Passions and other choral music, although Bach produced a world of music without words for worship.[21] Words accompanied by music help to direct a spirit. The church transmits the creedal faith about Jesus Christ through the poetry of hymns.[22] George Herbert, an Anglican divine, says of poetry,

17. Niebuhr, *Christ and Culture,* pp. 29-38.
18. Karl Barth, *Wolfgang Amadeus Mozart,* trans. Clarence K. Pott (Grand Rapids: Eerdmans, 1986). Barth tells us in this little book that he himself started his day by listening to Mozart's music.
19. Trans. John Bowden (Grand Rapids: Eerdmans, 1991).
20. See Edwards's sermon, "The Excellency of Christ," *Works of Edwards* (Worcester, Mass., 1808).
21. (Philadelphia: Fortress Press, 1986).
22. For a thorough, recent discussion of words and music of hymns, see Harry Eskew and Hugh T. McElrath, *Sing with Understanding* (Nashville: Church Street Press, 1995).

"A verse may find him, who a sermon flies / And turn delight into a sacrifice."[23] With this in mind, I shall dwell on the *words* of hymns and downplay the music, conscious that my readers will overhear some of the melodies when I refer to the words.

When we sing and hear hymns, versicles, antiphons, and responses we tap into the greatest repository of Christian teaching about Jesus Christ. They construct a portrait of Jesus and give us of the spirit of Jesus. So Paul advises the Colossians to sing psalms, hymns, and spiritual songs to God with gratitude in their hearts, that the word of Christ may dwell richly in them (Col. 3:16).

Such New Testament advice causes me to emphasize the importance of sung poetry over plain manuscripts. We sing a few hymns from the New Testament too. The "Gloria" in the Eucharist starts with the song sung by the choir of angels to the shepherds at the birth of Jesus, "Glory to God in the highest and peace to his people on earth" (Luke 2:14). Paul's Christological hymn in Philippians 2 invites us to let the mind of Christ dwell in us, since Jesus, "though he was in the form of God, did not regard equality with God as something to be exploited, but emptied himself, taking the form of a slave, being born in human likeness. And being found in human form, he humbled himself and became obedient to the point of death — even death on a cross" (Phil. 2:5-11). This is the Jesus with whom believers have acquaintance, the one who condescends to be human.

When asked to reduce the thesis of the formidable tomes of his great *Church Dogmatics* to a brief thesis, Barth reportedly declared, "Jesus loves me, this I know, for the Bible tells me so." This Sunday School hymn evokes memories of tender youth and innocent affection for Jesus Christ. The hymns we repeat with frequency make Jesus interactive.

The great requiems and masses of Verdi and Mozart tell the story of the Jesus of the church. Many of us join throngs of people at Christmas time for a sing-along of Handel's *Messiah*. But it occurs to me that these grand concert-hall performances must seem odd to postmodern concert-goers, who try to hear them purely as works of "high art." The analogy that comes to mind is the story of a busy

23. George Herbert, *Works: The Church Porch,* ed. F. E Hutchinson (Oxford: Clarendon, 1978), p. 6.

non-Christian Christmas shopper who, observing the Salvation Army soliciting funds in the name of the Christ of Christmas, turns indignantly to her companion. "How covetous these Christians are," she says. "They act as if Christmas belongs to them, as if they started it." It does. We did.

Main Street may act as if Christmas belongs to them, and some non-Christian concert singers may act as if the great classical religious compositions are merely grand music. But they are Christian music. The words, more than anything else, make them so. These universally appealing compositions triumph over cultural differences to tell about Jesus. They teach Christian theology. Their performances are occasions of evangelism which audiences pay high prices to hear.

When artists throughout the world sing Handel's "Hallelujah Chorus" with the words, "And he shall reign forever and ever," they are joining their voices to our theological affirmation that Jesus Christ is the Son of God, for God alone lives on forever. This dynamic inspires the joy of Jesus. Likewise, few compositions rival the profundity of Beethoven's "Ode to Joy," in his ninth symphony. Such works run the gamut of religious affections, which include our peace like a river, our joy like a fountain, our sense of the numinous, and our faith in the kingdom of God.

John Dominic Crossan's revolutionary may possibly find a few armchair devotees to talk about revolution, but it is not a bandit revolutionary who inspires "Jesus the very thought of thee with sweetness fills my breast" or the Gregorian chant that seeps into the soul. Similarly, St. Patrick's "Breastplate" has the words "Christ above me, Christ within me, Christ before me, Christ behind me" — categories that echo in the chapter headings of *Christ and Culture*.

Hymns fortify the faith of Christians even as they expound its theology. The verses and versicles may be good poetry or bad, but they teach the faith in a way difficult to extirpate from the heart. While it has been popular to argue that many churchgoers have not progressed beyond their Sunday School faith or their Confirmation preparation, I disagree. The words we sing enlarge our knowledge of Jesus and the Christian faith much more than we often realize. When we are younger we may be unaware of the significance of "O Word of God incarnate, O wisdom from on High." But when we're older we discover here teachings about the Incarnation, Scripture, and the Holy Spirit.

Hymns also transmit and preserve the teaching of Jesus as the archetypal Suffering Servant; their theology stands steadfastly behind this idea. While scholarly acceptance of Jesus as the Suffering Servant of Isaiah 53 has fluctuated through the years, his suffering on the cross is undeniable. As the black spiritual asks, "Were you there when they crucified my Lord?" Our presence there calls forth the sacrificial response to the suffering thus: "Were the whole realms of nature mine / that were a present far too small, / love so amazing, so divine, / demands my soul, my life, my all."

Hymns embody the essence of religion: praise and worship. We worship God through Jesus Christ, and we worship Jesus Christ the Son of God; not the moral teacher, not a bandit. St. Ambrose receives credit for elucidating this in composing the "Te Deum" ("We Praise Thee, O God, we acknowledge Thee to be the Lord"). It encapsulates a wealth of adoration.

On a more familiar level, many Americans still exult in "What a Friend We Have in Jesus." And as Bill Moyers explains on public television, our general experience of the grace of God through Jesus Christ causes most Americans to sing a hymn almost all of us know by heart, "Amazing grace, how sweet the sound / that saved a wretch like me. / I once was lost but now am found, / was blind but now I see." Former Washington mayor Marion Barry, once imprisoned for cocaine possession, made "Amazing Grace" the theme for a successful reelection campaign. Regardless of whether he did this for mere political gain or as a testimony of genuine personal change, he touched the hearts of ordinary people. "Amazing Grace" represents both the hope and the experience of radical personal and communal transformation, which gives us faith to believe that "We shall overcome some day" through Jesus Christ.

Like our Jewish brothers and sisters, Christians join together in singing the Psalms. For Christians, though, the imagery of Psalm 23 inevitably resonates with the words "I am the good shepherd" of John 10:11, and links us poetically to the figure of Jesus. Although the Five Gospels of the Jesus Seminar deny that Jesus spoke these words, the biblical image of Jesus as shepherd persists in our understanding of his essential character. Theologians and the church have continued to see the role of pastor through the image of shepherd. It is stamped again and again on our hearts every time we sing it. The church has the privilege of stating the faith. We need not become reactionary in responding to the Jesus Seminar, for the Jesus of the Creeds continues to inspire Christians to create great music about him, a music that invites everyone to sing.

Seeing Jesus

St. Paul believed that we behold the glory of God in the face of Jesus Christ (2 Cor. 4:6), and Christians down through the centuries have shared this conviction. Paul had a vision of this Jesus on the road to Damascus, and could claim like the other Apostles to have seen the Lord. Christians throughout the ages have made a similar claim. For most of us the claim is a figure of speech, but for many mystics and visionaries it is more than that. Christians have always found art and music indispensable for telling the world who Jesus is. Without these works, we present a truncated portrait of Jesus.

Temple Grandin, champion of the autistic, says quite simply, "I think in pictures. Words are like a second language to me."[24] A full portrait of Jesus requires pictures. People throughout the world have produced pictures of Jesus, and we continue to see him in these pictures. Imagination is indispensable to all knowing. Beauty and truth are inseparable. Sight provides insight to truth that the pictographical alone can represent. Richard Harries, Bishop of Oxford, tells us in *Art and the Beauty of God,* "We cannot separate considerations of beauty from either truth or goodness."[25] Since this conference attempts to explore the truth about Jesus, the beauty of Jesus has a place in our conversation. As the Icon of all icons, Jesus makes divine beauty known.

People frequently offer to paint us word pictures. In the past, many of us accepted this locution, a symbolic expression, at face value. But our world has moved beyond that. We are now very conscious that words are words and pictures are pictures. People cannot paint word pictures. Yet just as music helps us hear the inaudible harmonies of heaven — or as Keats so trenchantly phrased it, "Heard melodies

24. Temple Grandin, *Thinking in Pictures* (New York: Vintage, 1996), p. 19.
25. Richard Harries (New York: Mowbray, 1993), p. 104.

are sweet but those unheard are sweeter" — pictures, too, help us see the invisible through the visible. Keats made his discovery while contemplating the pictures on a Grecian urn.

The Jesus the church proclaims had physical features, for he became human in the Incarnation. This obvious truth often escapes us because we're accustomed to dealing with an abstraction. Yet we empathize with the motivation to present real pictures of Jesus; we have an urge to see representations of Jesus as the Suffering One. Isaiah warns us that the Suffering Servant has no comeliness that we should desire him. The well-known Small Crucifixion of Grünewald appeals to us because it shows us how the visage of Jesus was marred. When we encounter pictures of Jesus from various lands, we must look for the beauty our eyes can behold and try to see the spiritual beauty the pictures offer. More than inspection is required; participation is paramount. The pictures are all different, yet they possess some common spiritual features.

Although we all have some competence in obtaining truth from pictures, I would like to underscore four features of pictures that help us to appreciate them.

First comes color, which represents vitality and mood. Colors tell us of the mood of the artist at the time of a work's composition. They project the mood the artist wishes to evoke from those who look at the picture. Colors also present some of the artist's spirituality, something from within the artist's soul. The colors also communicate the artist's inner picture of the picture.

Form comes next. It represents the artist's appropriation of the physical world, the shapes of beauty. There is the simple beauty of a checkerboard pattern; there is the complex beauty of a landscape. But form can be difficult to decipher in abstract paintings. A conglomeration of unstable forms that merge into each other can intentionally represent chaos. We may see this readily in some abstract stained glass windows. Forms in stained glass windows and icons have given important openings for worship among Anglicans, Greek Orthodox, and Roman Catholics. They help to focus our minds and our beings.

Subject matter, be it a still life, portrait, or landscape, helps to discipline the judgment of what we see. Is the picture truly representative of what the artist claims? Portraits, for example, attempt to express the inner personality of the subject. People have been known to reject their portraits because, rightly or wrongly, their eyes disagree with the artist's eyes. This should make us cautious and reflective when we notice which features of Jesus a particular artist emphasizes.

Harmony provides a sense of completeness. The mixture of straight and curved lines in a composition informs our delight or distaste for a particular picture. Ill-composed pictures disturb us because they invoke a sense of incompleteness or displeasing dissonance. Well-composed pictures demand our approval.

Recalling again my graduate student years, in the early seventies white Americans argued with black Americans about what Jesus looked like. White Americans considered Jesus white, while black Americans insisted on a black Jesus. Having been raised in a culture where everyone knew what Jesus looked like, I found the disagreements unnecessary. I could have identified the portrait of Jesus in the dark. In the midst of all this, I bought a book, *Ecce Homo*,[26] in an Andover Harvard Library used book sale. It was a picture book. It so changed my view of the world that it has become an indispensable text in my teaching.

It shocked me to discover the variety of ways in which artists represented Jesus. Germans painted a Jesus with German features, the Chinese made him Chinese, Africans made him black, Indians gave him Indian features. Who could imagine a Jesus other than the one who resembles the Jesus of the Last Supper by Leonardo da Vinci? I was deeply embarrassed to discover that the Jesus I held dear all my life turned out to be Italian. I had not yet explored the glories of Rome but had been raised with pictures created by Italians such as Da Vinci, Michelangelo, Caravaggio, and Botticelli; Rembrandt and the Dutch Masters; Dürer and other Germans.

Pictures present historical dimensions of Jesus and historical understandings of who he is. The spirit of the pictures represents to us the beauty of God in the face of our Lord Jesus Christ. Obviously, the pictures call into question the one-dimensional Jesus of the Jesus Seminar. Differences in text, subtext, and context result in different portraits of Jesus. The wealth of pictures of Jesus illustrate my argument that the spirit of Jesus, more than his moral teachings, determines who he is.

26. Joseph Jobe, ed. (New York: Harper & Row, 1962).

Touching Jesus

"Who touched me?" Jesus asked, in the midst of a crowd. His disciples were affronted. How could he ask such a question among so many jostling people? But Jesus knew a particular woman's touch to be different. Touching the hem of his garment had healed her (Mark 5). He himself touched others to heal them. His touch healed the daughter of Jairus (Mark 5) and Simon Peter's mother. He touched a leper to heal him. People noticed. Many "begged to touch even the fringe of his cloak; and all who touched it were healed" (Mark 6:56).

Obviously, we are unable to touch Jesus physically because he is not with us in the flesh, but we, too, can come to know Jesus through touching him. The way we touch Jesus is through prayer. Distance makes no difference to the effectual touch of the same Jesus who lives on in the church. He continues to touch people directly. He is touched with the feelings of our infirmities, and he continues to heal bodies and souls. The healings of the body are physical, literal, and real. The healings of the soul and the mind are also real. Those who are healed report their transformation, and observers can tell the difference in their lives.

Jesus helps us to understand the significance of prayer to reach him through his own prayers. His prayers kept him in constant touch with God. He would rise early to find a place to pray. We do not know what he said on those occasions. Once he promised to pray for his disciples that they would overcome because "Satan has demanded to sift you like wheat" (Luke 22:31). He reinforces the example of his own prayer life by teaching his disciples to pray. The content of the Lord's Prayer demonstrates his understanding of what constituted appropriate prayer.

Jesus considered prayer a means of shaping the spiritual life. Since spirituality is the foundation of the morality he wanted us to practice, he taught morality in conjunction with our relationship with God. Morality inculcates virtue — right thinking and right behavior based on intelligible good principle. People can live morally upright lives without faith in God. Many virtuous persons who profess neither faith in God nor follow any formal religion nevertheless act aright on philosophical grounds such as humanitarianism.

Right action need not follow virtue, as Kant explained. Right

action may spring from prudence. Right action facilitates the peaceful
dwelling together in community, which we cherish irrespective of its
motivation. However, the several prayers of Jesus instruct us how to
remain in touch with God to do the good from the heart. This
understanding of the prayer life of Jesus helps to complete the list of
essential means through which the church knows Jesus. The one who
still touches and may still be touched is a rather different person from
the Jesus of the Jesus Seminar. Just as the Holy Spirit, his Resurrection, and his place in the Trinity make him different, so do his several
prayers. When we examine a few of them we discover significant
elements of his relationship with God.

They exemplify, for example, his unique status as Son of the
Father. He utters one of the briefest of his prayers at the tomb of
Lazarus. "Father, I thank you for having heard me. I knew that you
always hear me, but I have said this for the sake of the crowd standing
here, so that they may believe that you sent me" (John 11:42). The
Jesus Seminar voted against including this as an authentic prayer of
Jesus. This is quite consistent with its rejection of the canonical claim
that he said, "I am the resurrection and the life." However, the
memorable answer to this prayer lives on in the minds of believers in
the Resurrection. The prayer at the tomb assumes an affirmative
answer from God. It explains one of its purposes — Jesus prayed to
God for our sakes. He wanted us to believe in a particular kind of
God, one who hears prayer. He also wanted us to believe that he came
from God. Evidently, we can scarcely know Jesus fully unless we have
faith in prayer. Prayer precedes and accompanies believing.

We can hear repetitions of the same theme in the other prayers
of Jesus, prayers which give us insight into a wealth of concerns that
help us stay in touch with God through Jesus. Different occasions
determine the emphasis of the following themes:

(1) Unselfishness. We notice this in the prayer at Lazarus's tomb.
    Because Jesus wanted others to believe, he prayed for the sake of
    the crowd standing nearby.
(2) Intercession. This constitutes the core of the prayer of John 17,
    where Jesus prays for the preservation of the church in the world.
(3) Submission to God's will. The Holy Thursday prayer of
    Gethsemane brings into focus the protest of Jesus over God's

demand on him to die. He recognizes pain and suffering as a part of a living relationship with God. He submits.

(4) Honor of the name of God. The Lord's Prayer gathers up a wealth of concerns, including the three I have just mentioned. It contains a plea for forgiveness, for daily bread, and for the coming of the kingdom.

The Jesus Seminar rejects much of the Lord's Prayer as the words of Jesus but paradoxically admits his form of address to God in prayer as quite genuine. If the church were to approach the Scriptures as if Jesus and his immediate followers employed an amanuensis or two, it is very likely that their humanity would cause them to make a few mistakes. The words we possess may very well only approximate the exact terms Jesus used. But as Paul would say: "The letter kills, but the spirit gives life." Jesus touches us, and we remain in touch with him through the very Spirit who enables our prayers.

Conclusion

Becoming acquainted with the Jesus of the Christian tradition requires socialization and acculturation in the church. This is a principal way of knowing him. The accessibility of this Jesus has an important part to play in our believing in him. He differs from the Jesus of the Jesus Seminar in the significant ways I have outlined. We may see him, hear him, and touch him. Thomas Thangaraj quotes an Indian sacred poem containing sentiments that stand within walking distance of these ideas. It teaches that illumination is to behold the guru's sacred form, chant his sacred name, hear his sacred word, and ponder his sacred image.[27] I am trying to say much the same about Jesus, who is much more than the Indian guru who embodies true teachings. Jesus gives our life meaning because we believe he is "of one substance with the Father," and through his oneness with God he also makes us children of God. The Jesus Seminar seeks a different Jesus.

Other avenues of exploration into the life and person of the Jesus of the canonical Gospels remain open to us. The canonical Gospels

27. Thomas Thangaraj, *The Crucified Guru* (Nashville: Abingdon, 1994), p. 121.

themselves present different characterizations of Jesus. Matthew, Mark, and Luke know a slightly different Jesus; John knows a radically different one. We may also come to know Jesus through tasting his life in the Holy Communion, as a long and sacred tradition testifies.

We may also inquire into the ways Jesus ministered to children, whom he loved and appreciated. Accordingly it would be appropriate to explore definitive answers to questions as to whether children can know the Jesus of the Jesus Seminar and his impact on their spiritual lives. We know already that the Jesus Seminar fails to address the illiterate and the uneducated. We know that the Jesus of the Christian tradition welcomed the poor into the circle of his intimates both before and after his resurrection.

The Jesus Seminar follows the scholarly tradition of defining issues from a delimited perspective that ignores the significance of Jesus for women and minority peoples. Any renovated understanding of Jesus needs to take seriously their contribution to the life and persona of Jesus. The Jesus the church already knows has more character and kindness than the new Jesus the Seminar seeks. I would hope that as we all strive to enlarge contemporary knowledge and awareness of the persona of Jesus we will be drawn closer to the Person in whom dwells all the fullness of the godhead bodily.

Jesus and His Church

EDWARD L. SALMON, JR.

WHAT I'D LIKE to address in this essay is the notion of Jesus and the church. Jesus and his church. Jesus in the church. I think the church today is under judgment. I don't feel negative about being under judgment; in fact, I'm quite encouraged about it. I think that as we head into a new millennium, the shape of which we really don't know, we are in one of those hinge times in history, and we have a great opportunity in such a setting to reexamine our mission as a church to the world in which we find ourselves. I'd like to look at Jesus in the church in terms of this opportunity.

As I've had the privilege of traveling around the church as a Bishop, it has become obvious to me that our church is culturally divided. You don't have to be a genius to figure this out. Our church is divided almost as in the ancient debate between Protagoras and Plato. Protagoras insisted that humanity was the measure of all things, and Plato insisted that God was the measure of all things. Today we see this same struggle going on in the church. And the debates we're currently witnessing around the teaching of Jesus represent the sides of this struggle.

I have recently read two books entitled "Who is Jesus?" One was written by Robert Funk, the other by John Dominic Crossan. I read those books because I think it's very important to be aware of what is going on in other theological circles. I claim to be a somewhat orthodox Christian person. I think Fleming Rutledge says it well: "It was good enough for Paul and Silas, and it's been good enough for me." That doesn't mean we don't need to think and rethink all the time, but the ancient heritage of Christ crucified and resurrected is the firm foundation on which I ask God to give me the grace to stand.

As I read these two books it became clear that their underlying assumption was that the scholarship of the Bible, which once belonged to the churches, has now moved out into the secular institutions. These books also show that the Jesus Seminar approaches the Bible, and the Gospels in particular, as a cultural artifact rather than as an ecclesiastical handbook. In their historical research they actually begin by eliminating the literary structure of the Gospels. The goal is to dismantle the Gospel and discover the pieces that are authentic so as to find the real historical Jesus. The result, from my perspective, is to reduce all reality to history and all knowledge to historical knowing, as if reality had no larger framework.

If we are going to listen to what somebody has to say, we need to be careful to understand from whence they come. In Dr. Funk's book he concludes with 21 theses. Number 8, the thesis about Jesus, is particularly interesting. "We need to give Jesus a demotion," he writes. "He has asked for it. He deserves it. And we owe Him no less as the divine son of God centered co-eternal with the Father pending cosmic judge seated at God's right hand, he is insulated and isolated from his persona as the humble Galilean sage." This is how Funk sees Jesus, and what he has to say needs to be understood in this context. Dr. Funk concludes his theses by saying, "Here are my 21 theses. If I had a church, I would scotch-tape them to the door." Of course, the irony is that after you've read the theses you don't need a church anymore.

When I think about the writings of the Jesus Seminar, the first person in our own Anglican heritage that comes to mind is Bishop Spong. I should mention that Jack Spong and I have met on several occasions and are actually quite friendly. But we don't agree on much. In his book *Born of a Woman,* Bishop Spong gets things all figured out. The way he figures it, Mary was a teenage rape victim who got pregnant with an illegitimate child and was finally protected by Joseph. I don't think any comment is needed on this because there is certainly no evidence to support this kind of speculative thinking; but it tells you something about the reorientation or revisionism occurring, both in Spong's work and throughout the church.

A further example of this "new thinking" is Spong's understanding of Easter. He says that the Resurrection was not so much a supernatural external miracle as the dawning of an internal realization that this life of Jesus reflected a new image of God, an image that defied the conventional wisdom, an image that called into question the exalted King as the primary analogy by which God could be understood. The Resurrection is really just a mental adjustment by the first disciples.

Now I don't believe it's necessary to comment on that because I think we need to let it stand, and let thoughtful people think about it. My purpose is to point out that in our church there is a serious theological contingent attempting to rearrange who Jesus is. They are not accepting the integrity of the gospel proclamation, and they want to change it and replace it.

To add one final illustration of this kind of split, last summer the Center for Progressive Christianity sponsored a seminar at Trinity Cathedral in Columbia, South Carolina. What is interesting about that seminar is that they, too, had theses. The first thesis was that Jesus was *a door* rather than *the way* to the Father. They were deeply concerned about an attitude of toleration of other religious groups and, I believe, honestly trying to find ways to connect to a culture that is becoming more and more distant from any kind of understanding of the gospel tradition.

Now, as I look at these various positions, I don't find a lack of integrity. I don't find mean-spiritedness. What I find is what I believe to be a misunderstanding of the gospel. When we begin to think about the whole issue of toleration, the reason these positions fall short is that the benevolence bestowed and the toleration bestowed emerge from the bestower.

The problem in this new way of thinking, in our understanding of inclusivity, is that the benevolence is emerging from *us*. Benevolence and tolerance are by no means wrong. But I think we miss the point if we believe that we are the source of this benevolence. If humankind is the measure, then it is from that measure that the grace — whatever there is — will emerge. But if *God* is the source, then God is the One from whom that grace will emerge.

Inclusivity is a pathetic response to the sinful nature of humanity, to the gross nature of the human fall. Human benevolence simply cannot touch the depth of the problem, regardless of what a good heart we might think we have. And so as we look at our church and

Jesus in our church, I think we see these two very different theological cultures.

The Center for Progressive Christianity recently published a paper by Fred Plummer, who is the Senior Pastor of the Irvine United Church of Christ in Irvine, California. In talking about God in the Scriptures, he said, "I do believe that while God may not be comprehensible, God can be experienced. At least one can experience that which I choose to call God." He goes on to say that Scripture "is a collection of stories, metaphors, songs, and poetry which attempt to describe the indescribable, to give shape and form to what is otherwise the wind of the spirit. It is our choice based on our desire, if we want to have an experience or be in a relationship with that spirit. To do so means that we must write our own stories, create our own metaphors, sing our own songs. We must authenticate our own truth with our own experience."

Now that is not a thoughtless way of looking at things. It is not to say that there is no truth there, but it is to say that the source of the scriptural statement and the source of all reality is anthropic. It is human. It is not divine. It is horizontal. It is not vertical. Now you can certainly believe this with some personal integrity. But we as Christians cannot believe that this is the truth as we understand it, and we cannot let it define the nature of our community.

I think of two biblical quotations that stand in contrast to this way of thinking. One is the exchange with Pilate when he asks Jesus, "So you are a king." And Jesus answers him, "You say that I am a king. For this I was born, and for this I came into the world, to testify to the truth. Everyone who belongs to the truth listens to my voice." And Pilate asks him, "What is truth?" I see these two groups in the church trying to touch this same question.

But as Christians believe that *Jesus* is the truth. Thus Colossians says: "For in him all the fullness of God was pleased to dwell. And through him God was pleased to reconcile to himself all things, whether on earth or in heaven, by making peace through the blood of his cross."

Now with these two cultures in mind I believe the church is under judgment in our time. I think we are always under judgment and that Christ brings judgment to the church in a multitude of ways. One particular way I think the judgment of God is being experienced in the church today is by means of the context in which we find our-selves. It is certainly not the world in which you and I were born. It is a vastly different world. When I think about the early days of my life, the cultural context seems to have been what I would call a kind of benign Christianity. I'm not holding up the past as something necessarily good and promoting what we are experiencing now as something necessarily bad. This benign Christianity of my early days was a kind of public religion that had a way of anesthetizing the gospel, and that's always been a struggle for us. But it is to say that the world in which I grew up was friendly to the church. It may not have understood the gospel, but it was friendly to the church. The culture in which we live today is not friendly to the church. The media is not friendly to the church.

When I was Rector at a parish in St. Louis, for a few years in the spring semester I had the privilege of teaching a course in the English Department at Washington University. It soon became clear to me that in the academy there was a great deal of prejudice against Chris-tianity. If we don't understand this in the American academy today, we are simply deluded. The Christian church is beginning to experi-ence oppression. Not the kind of oppression that we see in other countries, which is the oppression of martyrdom, but a kind of op-pression in which the church is being gradually silenced. We need to be aware of this. We are living in a culture in which the old way of doing business doesn't work any more. Probably the old way of doing business *shouldn't* work any more. But I think one of the ways Jesus judges the church is by putting before us the challenges of a new day and a new age and by asking us how we're going to be faithful in this new day and new age.

I read recently that there are 10 million Mormons in the United States. There are not 10 million Episcopalians in the United States, and we were here a long time before the Mormons came along. There are 4 million Muslims in the United States today. A priest from the Diocese of South Carolina has told me that in Sumter, South Carolina, there is significant Muslim evangelism among the blacks of this com-munity, and it's making inroads. The world we live in is changing dramatically, and God is calling us to a new day — calling us to be faithful, calling us to look at who we are and how we handle the treasure of the gospel we've been given.

I think one of the places where we experience the judgment of God in our church today is in the way the church has formed itself. The government of the Episcopal Church was originally designed by John Locke. John Locke didn't think much of the church, but we are using his methodology. We also like to think of ourselves — with a House of Deputies and a House of Bishops — as a kind of government modeled after the government of the United States. Isn't that wonderful?

Here we are, a church with a cultural divide, where we have lived together in such a way as to witness against the gospel by the way we've treated each other, and we go to our general conventions and try to pass several hundred resolutions so the rest of the world will know how to behave. There is an irony in that. There is a judgment in that. If we Episcopalians can grasp the notion that we are no longer the establishment and that God has given us the task to proclaim the gospel, we might look at how we are ordered and ask the question in terms of the question Fleming Rutledge asks: "Will it preach?" And what I would say about our structure is: "Will it deliver or will it impede the gospel?" Those are questions we need to ask about the way we form ourselves as a church. If we gather together at General Convention and pray together and talk to each other honestly, instead of trying to outmaneuver each other, something just might happen. But it doesn't happen this way, and I believe God's judgment is that he will let us become what we do until we see ourselves in such need that we are able to do something else. I think it is time we rethink how we order our common life.

Now think about that in terms of our diocese or our parish churches. When you look at some of the struggles in our parish churches and you see some of the fights we get into in our parish churches, do you believe that six weeks of confirmation classes, with information about what it means to be an Episcopalian and the colors on the altar, prepare a person to be a disciple in this new age? I don't believe it does. I believe our intentions are honorable, but I think we are living in the past. Do you think that three sessions with a couple to be married will prepare them for holy matrimony? Do you think that what we call Christian education in many of our churches is going to be the kind of spiritual formation that sets a foundation in our children's lives that will last them a lifetime, a foundation on which they can build? I look at parish budgets when I make my rounds as Bishop, and I see that Episcopalians decline to invest in the spiritual formation of their children, because the amount of money spent in most parishes couldn't do that if your life depended on it.

When we look at our faith communities, we need to ask the question, as we move into this new millennium, as we live in a culture and breathe the air that is no longer friendly to the gospel, do we have a gospel-rooted people whose lives are transformed by the Cross and the Resurrection and can we share that with others? I believe that in some places we do, but we need to rethink how we live as the people of God in our congregations. We need to, and we are trying to, in a number of places, rethink this whole matter of leadership in our congregations. We don't need housekeepers in our churches. We need proclaimers. We need leaders who can make disciples who can make disciples. We don't need clergy who can just keep it all together in the ECW and keep the vestry from having a fight. We need people who can proclaim the gospel in such a way that lives are transformed and flow out into the communities where we live in ways that make a difference. We need to take seriously the ministry of the baptized. The whole understanding of lay ministry is a recent phenomenon in the church in the latter portion of this century. We're not talking about people to rake the yard and keep the church clean. We're talking about people as disciples carrying Christ to the world — carrying Christ to the community. We have not felt the need to do that in the past.

As I often visit congregations, I often find the notion afloat that everybody who's going to be an Episcopalian already is; they're already there in that church. We have many smaller congregations where there are wonderful, faithful people who have survived in that community as a small congregation and really believe that nobody else is needed there. Is that true to the gospel? Is that who we are as Christian people?

Episcopalians build beautiful churches. I can drive through almost any community in this country and usually spot the Episcopal church because it's tastefully done. That does not give us the privilege of worshipping it, but we do. The Baptists will tear a building down to build a bigger one. We wouldn't do that if our life depended on it.

Recently, I went back to Trinity Church in Natchez, Mississippi, where I was baptized and where my father and his mother and others before them were baptized. They were celebrating the 175th anniversary of the building of the parish church. The one thing that made the event particularly exciting for me is that when they built that church building in 1822, they had 22 members, and they built it to seat 500. There's something about this that reflects the heart of the gospel.

I think the travail we're experiencing in the church today is God's judgment to try to catch our attention — to try to get us out of the kind of management stance we're in, to realize how much we need God's grace and how much we need the gospel and how much we need each other.

The Commission on Human Affairs, which I have chaired this year, has on it the founder and the past president of Integrity, both of whom are good friends of mine. We don't agree on much. But agreement and what I would call godly care for each other are not mutually exclusive.

We have a good bit of sentimentality about relationships. I had a person say to me not too long ago that he was thinking about leaving the church. And I said, "Why is that?" And he said, "We have been in a fight, and I thought that the church was a place of brotherly love." He was a sort of chauvinist male, and he said, "I don't want to be in a church that's like what I've gone through." And I said, "Did you ever have a brother?"

What is this sentimentality that says everything is sweetness and light? God did not promise us sweetness and light. God didn't promise us that life would be without pain and without burden. God didn't promise us that we wouldn't have to think, that we wouldn't have to bear burdens for each other, that we wouldn't have to struggle, that life wouldn't have pain in it. He only promised to be with us, and he came to us on the cross in that pain. And it's that model which is the model of Christ's power in the church. Why would anybody want to join a group of people who are fighting and who hate each other? Why would they want to be there? I think that we could make a significant witness to the world if we could disagree with each other with integrity and with honesty and let God find ways for us to work through our differences and handle arguments. Now that would be a tremendous witness for people who don't agree — to believe that it's only the grace of God and the power of his Christ that can join us together.

But, you see, we have bought John Locke's model, and we believe that the way you have truth is that you get enough people to vote on it, and when they have decided, you run everybody else off. That is not a gospel community, and I believe that the Episcopal church today is under serious judgment because of the way we have been behaving.

As I've said elsewhere, we will not have any resolutions in the Diocese of South Carolina that vote on the uniqueness of Christ or that uphold God. We do not have a vote on that. It's the truth, and the minute you make a resolution out of it, you make it debatable. And so when strangers to the Episcopal Church read about our diocesan conventions — how we'll put something in a resolution, put it on the floor, have a terrible fight over it, and vote against the truth in order for another issue, which is not understood, not to be violated — these strangers really must wonder.

We need to rethink. I think God has humbled the Episcopal Church. The Episcopal Church is a sideline church today, whether we like it or not. In this culture, people do not look to the Episcopal Church. The only time we make the press is when we have a fight or when somebody does something wrong. There is nothing about the church in terms of what we stand for that this culture pays attention to. I believe that's God's judgment.

Timothy Sedgewick and Philip Turner wrote a book analyzing the pronouncements of the General Convention and the House of Bishops and basically said that they were an embarrassment. And they *are* an embarrassment because they are not producing thoughtful work. They are often politically motivated. There is not the kind of theological discernment that makes them worth hearing. We need to reform.

I think that when we look at Jesus' presence in the church today, we find ourselves under judgment. The Lord Jesus is saying to us, "how many more gross mistakes do you need to make before you realize your need to surrender?" I think the time for surrender has come. It is time to see what the Crucified and Resurrected One is saying to us, what opportunities are being offered to this wonderful church.

I want to emphasize that I am not discouraged about any of this. I happen to believe that God works out his purposes; it may be through pain and travail, but I believe his purposes will be worked out. As I've traveled around this church, I've seen vital congregations that are making a difference where they are, not only in the lives of their own people but in the communities where they're located.

In Memphis recently I talked to a priest named Colenzo Hubbard, a former lineman with the Alabama football team. Colenzo is not minuscule, as you might imagine. He has a parish church in the middle of the Memphis ghetto; and he told me that there are 1,500 families in the ghetto — 50 fathers, and lots of children. And one of the things I saw in that place was how this priest who understood what I call the burden-bearing of Christ was making a difference in the lives of those people and in the lives of those children. I saw how he was able to confront and work with teenage drug dealers, and turn their lives around. You see, that's a testimony to the resurrected Christ. And you see that all around the church. We don't hear about it very much, but it is happening. People are gathering at the foot of the cross, bearing one another's burdens, lives are saved, and the gospel is being lived.

I talked to a young woman some months ago who for five years had been involved in drugs. There was a prayer group in her parish church, and they started working with her and taking her in, and she's been dry now for three years. There is a group of people who have prayed for her every day, who have cared for her. Now that church is a community of transformation, a burden-bearing community.

We look around us in the culture, and we see people who are living together outside of marriage. And we say, "Well, people ought not to be living together." Quite often people who are living together are trying to find some kind of affirmation and love, and I don't believe they often find it in our parish churches. I don't think our parish churches are formed in such a way as to offer the life-transforming love we know in Christ. We have lots of activities, but if the church is to be a life-changing community, we will need to form our lives in such a way that this happens. The Holy Spirit of the Christ in whom we rest our lives is active and powerful in the church. I see that all over.

I was in a church this past Palm Sunday that for years had not done very well, and on that Sunday the new rector presented 70 people for confirmation. You see, it's not a large church, but things can happen. The Spirit moves, and when the Spirit moves, things happen.

In the *Living Church* recently there was a little article describing things going on around the Anglican Church. The writer said, "One diocese in Nigeria has confirmed 5,000 people a year for ten years. Are you aware that that is larger than most dioceses in the Episcopal Church?"

The *Episcopalian* had a front-page article that said of about 7,500 churches in the Episcopal Church, 5,690 were small. Now we ought not to give ourselves awards for that. We ought to be grateful for what we have, but we ought to take that as an opportunity to be more than that. And instead of saying, "That's what we ought to be," we ought to ask the question, "What does God want those churches to do?" Some of them he may want to stay small. I'm not suggesting that everything should be large. But we have a way of avoiding the gospel emphasis by saying, "Isn't it wonderful that we have 5,690 small churches?" And I want to say, "No, it's not wonderful. I'm glad they're there, but I think that God is asking all of us to do more than that."

The church in Uganda has set out to train 16,000 evangelists. Think about that. What is God calling us to do? Tanzania is a diocese that was formed in 1991, and there are now 59,000 communicants in that diocese. The Episcopal Church came to South Carolina in 1670, and we can rustle up about 27,000. I think that's a judgment. A million people are going to move to South Carolina over the next 20 years, and the judgment I think our diocese is under is: Will we be ready? Will we have the kind of leadership in our laity and our clergy that can take advantage of the precious gift that God is offering to us? I'm excited because I think Christ has humbled the church and is placing before us the opportunity to be disciples of the Crucified and Resurrected One.

In the same issue of the *Living Church* mentioned earlier there's a story about the Bishop of Mozambique, a man named Singulane whom I found so impressive. While the Bishop was waiting to board an airplane one day, a little five-year old girl sat down beside him. She saw his cross, and she said to him, "You must be one of those people who go to church. When the plane takes off, I would like to come and sit by you so that you can tell me what you know about Jesus, and I will do the same." After they were airborne, the little girl did sit down by the Bishop, and they shared experiences of Jesus.

"When we finished," said the Bishop, "she looked around and

saw a lady and turned to me and said, 'See that lady over there? She looks miserable. She may not know what you told me about Jesus Christ. I will go and tell her about Jesus.'" After a few minutes the girl returned to the Bishop and told him, "That lady was really miserable. She knew nothing about Jesus, but now she knows. I told her what you told me and what I knew."

That's Christian discipleship, and that's why I'm not worried about the church.

Jesus and the Eucharist

JOHN KOENIG

Introduction

The purpose of this paper is to discuss the practice, the meal, that lies at the very heart of our evangelical and Catholic worship and is dearly beloved by Anglicans. Increasingly, of course, this meal is called the Eucharist, though many still call it the Holy Communion or the Mass or the Lord's Supper. I would like to examine the Eucharist in order to gain greater clarity about how our Lord Jesus relates to the chief supper of the church. We tend to think that the issue has been long settled by clear passages from Scripture, but in contemporary biblical scholarship much is up for grabs, and so we have to re-ask many basic questions. When I first presented this paper, at the Cathedral Church of the Advent in Birmingham, Alabama, I felt much comforted by a great painting of the Last Supper fixed to the reredos of the altar behind me. The painting seemed appropriate, and perhaps more than coincidental. As in so many other churches, pictorial representations of the Supper like this one can help to draw us more deeply into sacramental worship. In this particular painting Jesus appeared to be speaking — probably uttering what we now call the words of institution. Unfortunately, a number of scholars now question whether Jesus really spoke such words, or whether there was a Last Supper at all. And these views need to be challenged.

From Jesus to the Eucharist

We can admit at the outset that Jesus did not "found the Eucharist" in any pure and simple manner. The chief ritual meal of the church was never seen by Christian believers through the centuries as a literal reproduction or reenactment of the Last Supper. Furthermore, the term "Eucharist," now popular among us, does not even occur in the New Testament. It first appears in a Christian writing called the *Didache,* close to the end to the first century; and then we find it several times in the writings of Bishop Ignatius of Antioch at the beginning of the second century. In the New Testament, the liturgical meal of the church based on the Last Supper is called by Paul the Lord's Supper, and sometimes, as in Acts, the breaking of bread. We have to allow for some kind of development between the Last Supper and even the earliest versions of that supper as it is commemorated in liturgy.

But then the question becomes: What kind of development? Did the historical Jesus give his disciples something to go on in establishing this supper as a regular ritual? If so, did they understand what he gave them? Did they properly follow out the implications of his ministry in their table worship? Was the development towards what we now call "Eucharist" in line with Jesus' intentions on the last night of his public ministry? Or — and this is the claim made by a number of contemporary scholars — did the church distort Jesus' intentions at the Last Supper? Even worse, did the church go so far as to invent the accounts of that Supper so as to make it seem that Jesus was the creative genius behind its community worship when in fact he was not? So our task centers on looking at what *kind* of development occurred from the Last Supper — if, indeed, it was a real historical event — into what we now call the Eucharist.

Jesus Christ at the Last Supper

The church could probably survive, and maybe even thrive, if irrefutable historical evidence were to show that there was no Last Supper, or that Jesus at some kind of final meal said farewell to his disciples but gave them no symbolic evidence that he saw himself as the Messiah who was about to die. But if that were the case, our faith and our liturgical practices would be much different. If we continued to use the *Book of Common Prayer* for our sacramental meals, we would have to admit that the words "This is my body. . . . This is my blood" were ecclesiastical metaphors for something — God knows what — because they never actually came from Jesus. Or perhaps we would celebrate our supper with the understanding that Jesus spoke these famous words but had no intention of using them as a pointer to his messianic vocation and his death.

It seems, however, that if we can demonstrate no meaningful continuity between the Jesus of history on the last night of his public ministry and the crucified and risen Jesus Christ, who is assumed by Paul to be present at the Lord's Supper, we find ourselves in an intolerable fix. We would always be open to the charge that the church's chief ritual meal is nothing more than self-invention, self-aggrandizement, self-promotion, and self-preservation. This is exactly the conclusion reached by the celebrated British novelist and biographer A. N. Wilson. I'm sure there are many reasons why Wilson now feels he can no longer call himself a Christian. But the reason for his disillusionment with the faith that is most poignantly articulated in his recent book on Jesus is what he takes to be the impossibility of showing that Jesus instituted the church's central ritual meal.[1] Wilson, an Anglo-Catholic at the time of this realization, experienced it as a huge blow. I think we would all suffer from a similar blow, even if we remained Christians.

On the other hand, if Jesus *did* mark his last night of freedom with a meal liturgy that was designed to highlight his sacrificial vocation as Messiah, and if he did this in such a way as to draw his disciples more deeply into that vocation; and if this particular symbolic act was vindicated by Jesus' resurrection from the dead, then the church's gospel takes on additional substance and authority. I'm going to argue that we can demonstrate, in at least a plausible manner, a straight-line development from the words and actions of Jesus Christ at the Last Supper to the Eucharist. The close connection between the terms "Christ" and "Last Supper" is extemely important. What I'm claiming is that Jesus knew of his messianic vocation on that evening and that

1. A. N. Wilson, *Jesus: A Life* (New York: W. W. Norton, 1992), pp. x-xi, 193-99.

this was, in large part, his reason for hosting a final meal with his followers.

A lot of people today doubt that. In particular, some strange and skeptical hypotheses have been generated by members of the Jesus Seminar, though I hasten to add that these scholars differ significantly one from the other, and they don't hold exactly the same position with respect to the Eucharist. Still, it is probably fair to say that most members of the Seminar tend to see the Eucharist as evolving from Jesus' practice of welcoming sinners and outcasts to meals with his disciples. Along with such scholars I take it to be a firmly established historical fact that Jesus was extraordinarily open to outcasts and marginal people and that this was a distinctive mark of his ministry, especially at meals. But should we agree with the Seminar consensus that this practice represents the real foundation for the chief ritual meal of the church, rather than a Last Supper at which Jesus intentionally symbolized his approaching death as Messiah with elements of bread and wine? I think not.

Hypotheses Generated by the Jesus Seminar

What positions do the Jesus Seminar scholars actually hold in this regard? As usual, John Dominic Crossan takes the boldest stance.

> What Jesus created and left behind was the tradition of open commensality [a sociological term that stands for Jesus' practice of eating with marginal people and social outcasts]. What happened was that, after his death, certain Christian groups created the Last Supper as a ritual that combined commensality from his life with a commemoration of his death. It spread through other Christian groups only slowly. It cannot be used as a historical event to explain anything about Jesus' death.[2]

You get the point. Crossan, as a practicing Catholic, would presumably affirm that the Eucharist remains an important part of the church's life. However, for him, the sacrament finds its original and chief

---

2. J. D. Crossan, *Jesus: A Revolutionary Biography* (San Francisco: HarperCollins, 1994), p. 130.

meaning in Jesus' welcoming practices, not in any last supper event associated with his impending death.

Another member of the Jesus seminar, Episcopalian Marcus Borg, offers a somewhat more cautious assessment of the traditional Christian view:

> We do not know if Jesus, in fact, held a last supper with his disciples at which elements of the meal, bread and wine, were invested with special significance. The stories of the Last Supper in the gospels may be the product of an early community's embryonic ritualization of the meal tradition rather than the historical recollection of the last night of Jesus' life.[3]

We might call this position thoroughgoing skepticism: one doesn't know and can't possibly know on the basis of the available evidence. Here we witness an interesting shift on the part of Professor Borg. In his earlier book, *Jesus: A New Vision,* he takes the view that Jesus probably did host a last meal with his disciples at which bread and wine were invested with symbolic value.[4]

A third position, a complex and imaginative one that I can only summarize, is held by Professor Bruce Chilton, who has sometimes participated in the Jesus Seminar.[5] Professor Chilton is an Episcopalian, a priest in fact, so he obviously places high value on the sacrament of the altar. But the meaning he posits for the Last Supper in relation to that sacrament is untraditional, to say the least. Chilton believes that Jesus presided over not one but a series of very distinctive meals following his provocative "cleansing" action in the Jerusalem Temple (see Mark 11:15-19), and that he did indeed speak words on the order of "This is my body. . . . This is my blood." But he did not mean by those sentences, which he uttered on more than one occasion, to found any sort of ritual practice that might be considered sacramental. In pointing to the bread and wine, Jesus was not talking about his own person; and he was not (here Chilton becomes emphatic) referring to the impending sacrifice

3. M. Borg, *Meeting Jesus Again for the First Time* (San Francisco: HarperCollins, 1994), p. 66, n. 35.

4. M. Borg, *Jesus: A New Vision* (San Francisco: HarperCollins, 1987), p. 188, n. 27.

5. R. W. Funk, R. W. Hoover, and the Jesus Seminar, *The Five Gospels* (New York: Macmillan, 1993), p. 534.

of his death. Instead, Chilton argues, Jesus was speaking of the bread and wine that, in line with his radical program of purity for the people of Israel, should be offered up to God by all Israelites in place of the current Temple sacrifices.[6]

This position is rather nuanced and deserves fuller elaboration and evaluation than I can present here. How, on this hypothesis, did the Last Supper come into existence? Chilton posits that after the resurrection — and he holds to the real occurrence of such an event — Peter took the lead within a group of Jesus' original disciples by idealizing one of the communal meals Jesus had hosted for them after the Temple incident. This then became in their minds a primal Last Supper, full of symbolic references to the Passover and Jesus' sacrificial death. It was this supper, a conflation of many experiences, that began to be commemorated regularly in the church's worship.[7] For Chilton, no single account of the Last Supper in the Gospels is close to being historically accurate, because each of them builds upon the fictional story fashioned by Peter and his circle in the early Jerusalem church.

The Origin and Transmission of the Bread and Cup Words

Where might we start if we wanted to present alternative hypotheses to those proposed by Crossan, Borg, and Chilton? I propose that we begin with a body of evidence that is seldom taken seriously by members of the Jesus Seminar, namely the writings of Paul. We know that Paul's ritual meal practice was centered in what he called the Lord's Supper. The clearest reference to this symbolic meal occurs in 1 Corinthians 11:23-26.

> For I received from the Lord what I also handed on to you, that the Lord Jesus on the night when he was betrayed took a loaf of bread, and when he had given thanks, he broke it and said, "This is my body that is for you. Do this in remembrance of me." In the same

6. B. Chilton, *A Feast of Meanings: Eucharistic Theologies from Jesus through Johannine Circles* (Kinderhook, N.Y.: E. J. Brill, 1994), pp. 63-81. See also Chilton's *Pure Kingdom: Jesus' Vision of God* (Grand Rapids: Eerdmans, 1996), pp. 85-90.

7. *A Feast of Meanings,* pp. 81-93.

way he took the cup also, after supper, saying, "This cup is the new covenant in my blood. Do this, as often as you drink it, in remembrance of me." For as often as you eat this bread and drink the cup, you proclaim the Lord's death until he comes.

You can see from this account that Paul is reminding his Corinthian readers of a tradition he has already given them in connection with the Lord's Supper. He begins with a kind of formula ("For I received from the Lord what I also delivered to you"), and only then does he go on to narrate the Last Supper. What contemporary investigators of the New Testament have learned from studying first-century Judaism is that in contexts involving tradition, like the one in 1 Corinthians 11, the words "received" and "delivered" function among rabbinic teachers as technical terms for the oral transmission of important truths.[8] On the rabbinic model, which Paul seems to be following here, the phrase "from the Lord" would probably denote not information revealed to the Apostle by the risen Christ but rather something transmitted to him by an individual who knew Jesus or by a chain of witnesses reaching back to Jesus. Within a rabbinic milieu the words "received" and "delivered" also indicate that care has been taken to preserve the content of the material in its various stages of transmission.

Paul writes his discourse on the Last Supper to the Corinthian church in about 53 C.E., and his founding visit to Corinth, during which he originally relayed the Last Supper tradition, occurred no later than 51 C.E. This means that we are looking at transfers of information that took place 20 years or less after the crucifixion and resurrection. When is Paul himself most likely to have received the meal story he passes on to the Corinthians? That transfer could have come as early as his reception into the church in Damascus, just after his conversion in the early thirties. At the very latest, I would say, Paul learned about the Last Supper tradition when he first journeyed to Jerusalem as a new believer. He tells us about this trip in his epistle to the Galatians:

> Then after three years I did go up to Jerusalem to visit Cephas and stayed with him for fifteen days; but I did not see any other apostle except James the Lord's brother. (Gal. 1:18-19)

8. G. D. Fee, *The First Epistle to the Corinthians* (Grand Rapids: Eerdmans, 1988), pp. 548f.

Here Paul relates that he went up to the Holy City for the express purpose of getting to know Peter[9] and that while staying at the home of this most important disciple he also met with James, perhaps unintentionally. It seems to me inconceivable that these two early leaders of the church, Peter and James, would have failed to elaborate upon the Jerusalem church's foundational worship practices for their guest, especially ritual meals associated with the life of Jesus himself. We should notice in this connection how Paul stresses the time frame of the story he has received: "the Lord Jesus on the night when he was betrayed, took bread. . . ." This is a self-consciously historical approach to narrative, right down to Paul's use of the simple name "Jesus," which he seldom employs without linking it to the title "Christ." For Paul and whoever told him this story, it was of great importance to locate the Last Supper on the final evening of freedom permitted to Jesus. I am suggesting, then, that Paul heard this historical account, with the words of institution included, no later than his first trip to Jerusalem as a believer. We can fix the date of that event from about 33 to 38 C.E.,[10] not very long at all after the Crucifixion and Resurrection.

Of course, Professor Chilton might chime in at this point by saying: "Yes, that's all well and good; but by the time Paul arrived in Jerusalem, even if it was just few years after the resurrection, Peter had already constructed his idealized Last Supper, and this was the tradition he passed on to Paul as fact." My first impulse here is to doubt whether an alleged Petrine circle could have convinced the entire body of Jesus' original disciples, some of whom were eyewitnesses to the last week of their master's life, that several events were really just one. However, to answer Professor Chilton more fully we can take a closer look at the Pauline words of institution: "This is my body. . . . This cup is the new covenant in my blood." These words come across as provocative no matter what interpretation we place upon them. To some first-century Jews who were invited to eat and

9. E. Krentz, *Galatians,* Augsburg Commentary on the New Testament (Minneapolis: Augsburg, 1985), p. 32.

10. R. Jewett, *A Chronology of Paul's Life* (Philadelphia: Fortress, 1979), pp. 29f.; M. Hengel and A. M. Schwemer, *Paul between Damascus and Antioch: The Unknown Years* (Louisville: Westminster/John Knox, 1997), pp. 26f..

drink elements so blessed by Jesus, the specter of cannibalism must have threatened (John 6:52ff.). The institutional words are strange indeed, and yet if they came to Paul through a chain of tradition originating with Peter in Jerusalem, and as early as we have posited, there is virtually no possibility that Hellenistic ideas about the ritual consumption of a god slipped in to shape the words, thereby creating a practice alien to Judaism. Historically, we are dealing with a Palestinian Jewish process, and a brief one at that. Almost certainly, Jesus himself spoke the provocative words or something close to them. Yet this high probability simply magnifies the prior question: How could Jews of the first century understand Jesus' symbolic utterances as anything other than offensive? Is Professor Chilton's explanation of what Jesus intended by them correct after all? I don't think so.

Rabbi Lawrence Hoffman, who serves as Professor of Liturgy at New York's Hebrew Union College, addressed the issue of Jesus' intent at the Last Supper almost twenty years ago in an article written for the Christian journal *Worship*. In that article Professor Hoffman argues that Jesus' bread and cup words, while bold, would have found comprehending hearers among many first-century Jews. This would be the case particularly with regard to the bread utterance, "This is my body." Hoffman contends that even before the Temple's destruction in 70 C.E. Jews were beginning to associate the bread of the Passover meal, the *matzah,* with the Passover lamb.[11] So Hoffman is telling us in effect that when Jesus took the *matzah* in his hands and said "This is my body," at least some of his disciples, along with other first-century Jews, would likely have concluded: "Oh God, he's talking about the paschal lamb; and if he's comparing himself to that lamb, he's forecasting some terrible event in which he is to give up his life as a sacrifice."

Hoffman also finds in Jesus' words over the cup a sacrificial meaning pointing to his death, though he does not argue this point at length. What we can add to his thoughts is that any equation implied by Jesus between his blood and the wine, or between his blood and God's covenant with Israel,[12] would sharpen the allusion to his im-

11. L. Hoffman, "A Symbol of Salvation in the Passover Haggadah," *Worship,* vol. 53, no. 6 (1979): 519-37.

12. We cannot be absolutely certain whether Jesus used the term "covenant" (Mark 14:24) or "new covenant" (1 Cor. 11:25) when referring to the cup of

pending death. Even the unlearned disciples, already alerted by Jesus' bread words to the probability of his death, would have heard echos in his cup words of well-known scriptures like Exodus 24:8, where Moses says of the oxen sacrificed at Mount Sinai at the giving of the Torah, "See, the blood of the covenant that the LORD has made with you." At the very least, Jesus' table companions would have begun to visualize blood gushing from the sacrificial animals whose slaughter they had observed in the Temple. Professor Chilton's thesis regarding the bread and cup words, which understands them as Jesus' advocacy of a substitute for animal sacrifices, without any reference to his death, only works if it can be established that Jesus taught his alleged program of purity in isolation from the charged atmosphere of Passover, with its focus on the sacrificial lamb. But the firm historical record of Jesus' last days in Jerusalem during Passover week renders such a reconstruction highly improbable.

In summary, then, we can put forward very solid evidence for the traditional view that Jesus spoke bread and cup words like the ones recorded in our New Testament accounts at a final supper with his disciples on the evening of his arrest. Furthermore, we can assert with some confidence that in speaking these words Jesus intended to symbolize his approaching death and was calling his disciples to share his sacrifice in a very physical way by their eating and drinking. All of this, though considerably more than Crossan, Borg, and Chilton would allow, should be seen as a bare minimalist interpretation of the Last Supper.

The Place of the Last Supper in Jesus' Public Ministry

Before moving on to what else we can know about the Supper, we should note that our minimalist reading is supported by an additional body of evidence, and quite a large one at that. It consists of words and deeds from Jesus' ministry prior to his last days in Jerusalem,

---

wine. The more difficult reading, and therefore the one likely to be earlier, is the simple "covenant." As the church continued to pass on traditions about Jesus, it tended increasingly to emphasize the newness of his work and to cite or allude to Jeremiah 31:31.

plus two events that took place during those last days just before the Supper. In brief, most scholars have concluded that something very much like the Last Supper narrated by Paul and the synoptic Evangelists would have formed an appropriate, if not inevitable, finale to Jesus' public ministry. The whole category has been effectively analyzed in recent works by E. P. Sanders, J. D. G. Dunn, and N. T. Wright, and I need highlight only one aspect of the words and deeds referred to.[13] For our purposes, the overall characteristic of the relevant material is the way in which images of eating and drinking predominate, especially in Jesus' sayings about the kingdom and his prophetic enactments of it.

Consider just a few of Jesus' better-known pronouncements from the synoptic Gospels. In Luke's version of the Beatitudes, for example, we read: "Blessed are you poor, for yours is the kingdom of God. Blessed are you that hunger now, for you shall be satisfied" (Luke 6:20f.) — presumably in the kingdom. Similarly, in Luke's wording of the Lord's Prayer, which many scholars take to be closest to Jesus' original utterance, we find two familiar petitions sequenced in a way different from the Matthean version of the prayer that is the basis for our everyday church usage. Luke has Jesus pray: "Thy kingdom come. Give us this day our daily bread." The clear implication of juxtaposing the petitions this way is that the coming of the kingdom and bodily sustenance somehow belong together. As for the final coming of the kingdom, we find that Jesus declared: "Many will come from east and west and will eat with Abraham and Isaac and Jacob in the kingdom of heaven" (Matt. 8:11; see also Luke 13:28f.). Here the primary image for the kingdom in its completed form is that of a great feast, a picture that Jesus probably derives from passages in Isaiah and Zechariah:

> On this mountain the LORD of Hosts will make for all peoples a feast of rich food, a feast of well-aged wines, of rich food filled with marrow, of well-aged wines strained clear. And he will destroy on this mountain the shroud that is cast over all peoples . . . he will swallow up death forever. (Isa. 25:6f.)

13. E. P. Sanders, *Jesus and Judaism* (Philadelphia: Fortress, 1985); *The Historical Figure of Jesus* (Allen Lane: Penguin, 1993); J. D. G. Dunn, *Jesus' Call to Discipleship* (Cambridge: Cambridge University Press, 1992); N. T. Wright, *Jesus and the Victory of God* (Minneapolis: Fortress, 1996).

Thus says the LORD of Hosts: I will save my people from the east
country and from the west country. . . . On that day the LORD their
God will save them, for they are the flock of his people. . . . Grain
shall make the young men flourish, and new wine the young women.
(Zech. 8:7; 9:16f.)

Comparable images of the kingdom as feast occur, sometimes explicitly and sometimes by implication, in Jesus' parables (Mattt. 22:1-10;
25:1-13; Luke 15:11-32; 16:19-31). Furthermore, when speaking of
his own vocation as Son of Man, which is closely related to the coming
of God's kingdom, Jesus answers his critics as follows: "For John [the
Baptist] came neither eating nor drinking, and they say, 'He has a
demon'; the Son of Man came eating and drinking, and they say, 'Look,
a glutton and a drunkard, a friend of tax collectors and sinners!'"
(Matt. 11:18f.). The idea here seems to be that Jesus' opponents think
he spends too much time at table, to the point of overindulgence —
plus, he has the wrong kind of friends. And Jesus is half admitting
that it's true, isn't he? At least the gospel writers think so, because on
several occasions they portray our Lord and his disciples eating, even
feasting, with marginal folk and those whom society generally con-
demns as unrighteous (see especially Mark 2:15ff. with its synoptic
parallels and the story of Zacchaeus in Luke 19:1-10).[14]

So Jesus' ministry as a whole exhibits this quality of celebration,
often at table; and at the same time his actions preview an even greater
celebration in the final coming of God's kingdom. Indeed, we have
to imagine that when people saw Jesus eating with tax collectors and
sinners, as well as those generally acknowledged to be good citizens
(Luke 7:36ff.; 14:1ff.), they frequently saw him doing this in the
company of his twelve disciples. That kind of scene would have
excited messianic hopes among first-century Jews because the number
twelve stood for the tribes of Israel, mostly dispersed and assimilated
in Jesus' day, but expected by many to reappear with their original
family characteristics when God acted decisively at the end of time to
rescue his chosen people from their oppressors. Here again Jesus
anticipated the final feast of the kingdom. Our gospel accounts of the

14. For the historical reliability of Matthew 11:18f. and Mark 2:15ff., see
J. Koenig, *New Testament Hospitality* (Philadelphia: Fortress, 1985), pp. 20-26.

Last Supper would seem to be in perfect alignment with Jesus' ministry as a whole and could easily have been seen as its most fitting climax. It makes sense for Jesus to have said farewell to his disciples with just such a meal.

Two of Jesus' last symbolic acts, though not directly related to feasting, fill out the picture of our Lord as one who was intentionally symbolizing the imminence of the kingdom. When we place them together in a triad with the Last Supper (for they all occurred within a few days of one another), they provide a common witness to Jesus' understanding of himself as a unique agent of God. The two acts I am referring to are Jesus' entry into Jerusalem on a donkey, surrounded by psalm-singing followers, and his provocative behavior in the temple, which is sometimes called the "temple cleansing" but may be more accurately described as an enacted forecast of the Temple's destruction. Both of these events — and the Last Supper too, in its connection with Matthew 8:11 and Exodus 24:8, evoke memories of the prophet Zechariah, some of which were interpreted messianically in the first century.

Scholars of the Jesus Seminar, along with some other contemporary scholars, would have us believe that Jesus himself did not mean for those observing his ministry to think of explicit passages from the prophets when he acted. In fact, a number of such scholars doubt that the festal entry into Jerusalem, as recorded in our Gospels, happened at all. Instead, they hold that the early church fashioned this event from its postresurrection reflections on Zechariah 9:9. On this score I find the work of Sanders, Dunn, and Chilton to be more historically sound. All three scholars argue, in varying degrees, that Jesus consciously acted according to prophetic paradigms,[15] which means that when he said or did something unusual, he probably intended that his followers (and enemies!) should catch his biblical allusions and use them to draw conclusions about his mission. Clearly, we should apply this line of reasoning to our understanding of the Last Supper. In my view, all streams of evidence lead toward the conclusion that Jesus actually hosted such a meal and that he meant it to be highly symbolic of his identity and vocation.

15. Dunn, *Jesus' Call to Discipleship,* pp. 92-100; Sanders, *The Historical Figure of Jesus,* pp. 241-64; Chilton, *Pure Kingdom; Jesus' Vision of God,* pp. 13, 82, 85.

The Messianic Meaning of Mark 14:25

With this background we can now move beyond a minimalist interpretation of the Last Supper to explore one of the strangest passages
in the gospel narratives of the meal. According to Matthew, Mark, and
Luke, Jesus linked his words over the bread and wine with some form
of the saying: "I will never again drink of the fruit of the vine until
that day when I drink it new in the kingdom of God" (Mark 14:25).[16]
Why is this saying so odd? First of all, it looks like a vow of abstinence
from wine, which seems highly uncharacteristic of Jesus in the light
of judgments leveled against him that he was a glutton and a drunkard.
Second, although Jesus here promises, by implication, that he *will*
drink new wine (or drink wine in a new way) at the final coming of
the kingdom, presumably in the course of a great feast, the New
Testament never shows us any images of Jesus doing this. After his
resurrection, our Lord eats and drinks with the disciples, but textual
references to these occasions give us no indication that wine was ever
involved. In other words, Mark 14:25 represents an unfulfilled prophecy, and that fact alone argues for the saying's authenticity since New
Testament writers always try to demonstrate the accuracy of Jesus'
prophecies.[17] In this case, they felt bound to preserve a difficult saying
that was not very useful to them, most probably because everyone
knew that it had actually originated with Jesus. Third, because even
the earliest church seemed puzzled about just what to do with Jesus'
prophetic vow, liturgists tended not to incorporate it into services of
eucharistic worship. I know of no such usage in our Western churches.

John Meier, one of many commentators who take Mark 14:25 to
be authentic, lays stress on its promise aspect.[18] Jesus, Meier believes,
is emphatically stating that the feast of the kingdom will occur and
that he will be there to enjoy it. So the statement functions to counter-
balance the sober references in the bread and cup words to Jesus'
death. "My sacrifice," Jesus seems to be saying, "will be met with

16. See J. P. Meier, *A Marginal Jew: Rethinking the Historical Jesus,* vol. II (New
York: Doubleday, 1994), pp. 302-9, for convincing arguments as to the priority of the
Markan words in the synoptic tradition.

17. Another mark of the passage's authenticity is its coherence with Matthew
8:11.

18. Meier, *A Marginal Jew,* pp. 308f.

God's enthusiastic approval at the great feast." Moreover, the vine to which Jesus refers is a favorite symbol of abundance in Jewish expectations of the age to come. The promise of feasting on Mount Zion in Isaiah 25:6-8, which Jesus almost certainly envisioned when he spoke the words recorded in Matthew 8:11, presupposes this image of the luxuriant vine; but we can also point to more explicit references (*Did.* 9:2; John 15:1-11; *2 Bar.* 29:5-6).

One Old Testament passage in which the vine of the new age figures prominently has, I believe, suffered underutilization in efforts to interpret Jesus' words at the Last Supper. I suspect that Jesus was intentionally alluding to it when he uttered the words of Mark 14:25. The passage in question occurs in Genesis 49 as one of the blessings spoken by Jacob over his twelve sons, the prototype-founders of Israel's tribes. The blessing invoked upon Judah, the tribe from which King David and Jesus came, reads as follows:

> 10) The scepter shall not depart from Judah, nor the ruler's staff from between his feet, until tribute comes to him; and the obedience of the peoples is his. 11) Binding his foal to the vine and his donkey's colt to the choice vine, he washes his garment in wine and his robe in the blood of grapes; 12) his eyes are darker than wine, and his teeth whiter than milk.

This passage prefigures the prophecy in Zechariah 9:9 about a messianic king riding on a donkey's colt and is therefore of a piece with Jesus' symbolic entry into Jerusalem. Thus we need not be surprised to learn that Genesis 49:11ff. was interpreted messianically at Qumran, that is, in at least one group of religious Jews contemporary with Jesus.[19]

But we should not fail to notice an element of this passage that might well have embarrassed the early believers and may account for the nonusage of Mark 14:25 in the church's liturgical meals. What I mean is the rather heavy hint in this passage that the messianic figure of the age to come celebrates exuberantly, and even wildly — that he overindulges. The Hebrew text of v. 12 can be translated: "his eyes shall be red [bloodshot] with wine" (RSV); and the Septuagint Greek

---

19. J. Koenig, *New Testament Hospitality,* p. 50, n. 45.

text which was known to most Jews of the first century can only read: "his eyes are glazed from wine."

How shall we put all of these data together? I would argue that in Mark 14:25 Jesus is speaking primarily about his own fate as a suffering and dying Messiah who will receive his vindication at the future feast of the kingdom. He does not speak in the Markan version about a reunion with his disciples (contrast Matt. 26:29). Instead, his point has to do with his role as a trailblazer for others — through the dark valley of death and into the abundance of the kingdom. He is the forerunner Messiah who will initiate the feasting; and that feasting will prove so joyful that only words of riotous excess can begin to describe it. Jesus' vision of his celebration "in the kingdom" gives him strength to complete his sacrificial vocation.

If we accept this interpretation as probable, there can be little doubt that Jesus was directed by a messianic consciousness when he called his disciples together for a last meal, a meal that was at once both deeply solemn and intensely hopeful. Of course we may doubt that the disciples who gathered at table with Jesus on that night, confused and frightened as they were, were able to comprehend what their master intended to symbolize. Only in the new atmosphere of the resurrection would they begin to savor the fullness of the meal's implications.

The Last Supper Shapes the Lord's Supper

In his longest discourse on what he has come to call the Lord's Supper (1 Cor. 11:17-34), Paul does seem to comprehend the unique blending of sacrifice unto death with kingdom abundance that characterized Jesus' message at the Last Supper. It may well be that the early disciple who passed on the Last Supper tradition to Paul (most likely Peter) was responsible for tutoring him in this perspective. In any case we can assume that at some stage in the life of the Jerusalem church prior to Paul's conversion the Last Supper was already being commemorated liturgically, on a regular basis. Paul gives no indication that he invented the ritual he calls the Lord's Supper, and there is one passage indicating that he expects it to be celebrated in the gentile church of Corinth each Saturday night (1 Cor. 16:2 in the light of

11:23). Such a weekly rhythm would argue for an origin among Jewish believers, who could well have seen the ritual as both a fitting conclusion to the Sabbath and an honoring of the Lord's resurrection early on Sunday morning (see also Acts 20:7-12).[20]

How, specifically, does the Last Supper tradition received and passed on by Paul shape the practice of the Lord's Supper — or rather the optimum practice of that supper as expounded by the apostle for his Corinthian readers? First, Paul clearly believes that the Lord's Supper is a messianic feast. It is the Lord Jesus who presents himself in the eating and drinking done by Christ's body, the church. Above all, it is the ecclesial body of the Messiah that must be discerned in the Supper (1 Cor. 11:29). Second, the sacrificial and vicarious death of Jesus takes center stage in the Pauline Lord's Supper (11:23-27). Indeed, the Apostle's only direct commentary on the words of institution goes this way: "For as often as you eat this bread and drink the cup, you proclaim the Lord's death until he comes" (1 Cor. 11:26; the words "until he comes" anticipate a description of Christ's coming in glory in 15:20-28 and may be derived from Paul's knowledge of Jesus' visionary vow in Mark 14:25). Third, as at the Last Supper, so in the Lord's Supper those who eat and drink participate in a boundary event in which the kingdom or age to come impinges so powerfully on the present moment that a transformation of life occurs (see 1 Cor. 10:11 in the light of 15:24). For Paul, living on the resurrection side of Jesus' life and ministry, this transformation discloses itself most dramatically in the sharing of spiritual gifts for mutual ministry (1 Cor. 12–14) — and precisely within the context of worship at table.[21] Almost certainly such commemorations of the Last Supper, in combination with manifestations of spiritual gifts, took place prior to Paul's conversion, probably in the Jerusalem congregation (Acts 2:1-42; Rom. 15:27). Here, as on the night of Jesus' arrest, sacrificial death is commingled with an experience of God's gracious abundance.

20. Jews of Jesus' time considered the day to end at sundown. Hence our "Saturday night" would be "Sunday morning" to them.

21. For evidence supporting the view that chapters 11–14 of 1 Corinthians refer to a single worship event, see C. Jones in *The Study of Liturgy*, rev. ed. (New York: Oxford University Press, 1992), pp. 193, 206, n. 19. Most recently, B. Lang has made this same case in his *Sacred Games: A History of Christian Worship* (New Haven; Yale, 1997), pp. 372-78.

Clearly, the Lord's Supper represents no simple reproduction of the Last Supper. In the Lord's Supper Jesus is known as crucified and risen, with the result that a whole new consciousness has been granted to those who eat and drink of the blessed elements. Yet we can identify real continuity between the two suppers, and we can speak of the second as an authentic development of the first. It even makes sense to assert that Jesus, through the interplay of his Last Supper words and deeds, his risen presence in the church, and the power of the Holy Spirit that he bestows, has "founded" the ritual meals celebrated by his earliest followers. And of course it is from these ritual meals of the New Testament era that our own Eucharists have evolved.

The Eucharistic Gifts and Claims of Jesus Christ

What happens at the Eucharist? We can never answer that question definitively because attempting to do so would place limits on our risen Lord's creative fashioning of blessings in bread and wine for his followers throughout the centuries. The truth is, the meaning of the Eucharist keeps expanding, as indeed it should within the framework of an incarnational faith that takes history seriously. And yet, if we understand the table worship of the New Testament believers to be somehow normative for us and productive of our own experience, then we can say something about the foundational role of the Last Supper and Lord's Supper in our own eucharistic practice.

Above all, we may affirm that what happens at eucharistic meals deriving from the Last Supper and the Lord's Supper is a unique, numinous sharing in the work and destiny of the Messiah Jesus. This is something Jesus desires. On that last night of his public ministry he feels the need for company with his disciples as he is about to go the way of the cross. They do not understand very much; they offer him little or no comfort. But according to his vision of God's plan they must be there, not only as witnesses but also as participants in his unfolding mission. In ways they cannot comprehend, through bread and wine they share in his death, resurrection, and future feasting. So also it is with us.

But this view of the Last Supper leads us to the further conclusion that every time we eat and drink of the Eucharist we enter more deeply into God's saving acts *for Israel.* The Eucharist always retains an old covenant flavor, and a good one at that. In Mark's version of the institutional words, which are probably closest to Jesus' original words, our Lord says: "This is my blood of the covenant" (14:25). We must read that as a pronouncement that harks back to the giving of the Torah on Mount Sinai (Exod. 24:3-8; Zech. 9:11) and as an assurance by Jesus that the ancient covenant still stands. Even when we accent new covenant language in our Eucharists, which most of our liturgies do, following the Pauline words of institution in 1 Corinthians 11:25, we are still bound to join the experience of Israel in its yearning for the fulfillment of prophecies by Jeremiah (31:31-34) and Ezekiel (36:24-27). Every celebration of the Eucharist thus becomes a Jewish-Christian event, a reminder to us of our special relationship with God's original chosen people. We, as gentile guests of Israel's Messiah, become necessary actors in the renewing of God's ancient covenant.

What the Last Supper, the Lord's Supper, and the Eucharist all offer us is a bodily sharing, through Jesus' messianic presidency, in God's covenantal redemption of the world. To be sure, we receive blessings and strengthenings of our individual lives at the Eucharist. But the greatest gift and challenge that comes to us through our Holy Communion with Jesus is a fuller incorporation into God's cosmic plan of redemption — or as Paul calls it in 2 Corinthians 5:16-21, the "ministry of reconciliation."

The central message of the Last Supper, which persists into our own Eucharists, is one of promise. This meaning comes through most clearly in Mark 14:25, where Jesus foresees his own celebration at the kingdom feast. But the atmosphere of Jesus' final meal with his disciples, and of our own meals, is altogether communal; and so therefore is the hope they convey. Jesus prophesies and goes on his way to the cross — for his disciples, for Israel, and ultimately (since he interpreted his work in terms of Isa. 25:6-8) "for all peoples." The presence of Jesus and the world-embracing promise of God belong together — always. But it is the Last Supper, coming to mind again and again in the communal meals of the early believers, and in our meal liturgies, that most powerfully conveys this saving unity. We do not go wrong, then, to claim that in a very real way Jesus both founded and continues to found the church's Eucharist.

Galilee Moments: Witnesses to Jesus' Resurrection, the Disciples, and the Revival of Vocations and Ministries

GUY FITCH LYTLE III

O sons and daughters, let us sing!
The King of heaven, the glorious King,
o'er death and hell rose triumphing.
Alleluia, alleluia!

That Easter morn, at break of day,
the faithful women went their way
to seek the tomb where Jesus lay.
Alleluia, alleluia!

An angel clad in white they see,
who sat and spake unto the three,
"Your Lord doth go to Galilee."
Alleluia, alleluia!

That night the apostles met in fear;
amidst them came their Lord most dear,

This explanation of Sewanee's new program is based on my lecture at the Anglican Institute's Conference, "The Truth about Jesus," at the Cathedral Church of the Advent in Birmingham, Alabama (April 1997).

and said, "My peace be on all here."
Alleluia, alleluia!

On this most holy day of days,
to God your hearts and voices raise,
in laud and jubilee and praise.
Alleluia, alleluia!

(Hymn 203, *Hymnal 1982*)

DRAWING ON THE SCENARIO described in this wonderful old Easter hymn, I want to introduce a practical component to our theological reflections on the truth about Jesus. As important as it is to know the truth about Jesus, it is also important to embody that knowledge in our wills, in the way we live as disciples and apostles. So I want to describe a new program focused on intellectual honesty, spiritual reflection, and vocational nurture that I hope will be of some benefit to the church and its clergy. This program, designed at Sewanee, is called "Galilee Moments." You will see, as I describe some of the practical and theological background of this program and give you a sense of what it hopes to accomplish, that "Galilee Moments" has an immediate relevance to a belief in the centrality of Jesus to our faith and lives even as the cultural and social environment around us goes through almost unfathomable changes.

Several years ago I published an article entitled "The Crisis of Identity in the Priesthood and the Revival of the Church."[1] In that article, I discussed the condition of the priesthood currently in the Episcopal Church and called for some necessary reforms. Perhaps with some hubris on my part, but also I believe with accuracy, I set my argument in the framework of John Henry Newman's *Tract I*, where Newman called the Anglican clergy of 1833 to recognize that the times were generally bad for religion and that the situation of those in holy orders was intolerable. He challenged the clergy to remember the high road of their calling and responsibility and to accept that it

---

1. *Sewanee Theological Review* 38:3 (Pentecost 1995): 227-40.

was time to do whatever they could to remedy this situation. That tract, along with Keble's Assize sermon in Oxford, marked the beginning of the Oxford Movement, an important moment in the revitalization of Anglicanism and Christianity as a whole.

I think we — both the clergy and the church as a whole — are indeed in a parallel situation now, and it is time that *we* remember our vocations and responsibilities and try to respond in appropriate ways. I do not intend to repeat the analytical and rhetorical points of my earlier article. Some of its assertions were intentionally overstated and some are open to argument; but the general thrust has been confirmed over and over. In fact, new challenges to the priesthood have emerged since I wrote. All indications now point to a seriously burgeoning clergy shortage in the Episcopal Church. Everywhere there is more debate, both theologically and practically, about such things as full-time ordained ministry "positions," Canon 9 ordinations, lay presidency at the Eucharist, etc. Some are even asking who needs priests, especially trained priests? For many, they are just an expensive, even oppressive, archaism. In 1995, Elisabeth Schüssler-Fiorenza, the well-known feminist theologian at Harvard, was invited to address a conference of Roman Catholic women seeking ordination. She stunned her audience by telling them that their project was quite wrongheaded, that they should not be seeking ordination; rather, they should be working to abolish the priesthood, the creation of which was a mistake in the church's history and part of its patriarchal hierarchy. I hasten to say that most of the conference participants did not agree with her, and they have continued to meet and press their cause.[2]

While there are many, many dedicated, hard-working, even happy, Episcopal clergy doing wonderful ministries throughout the church, considerable sociological evidence and psychological studies show that we clergy at the present time are in many ways facing real and potential trouble. We have problems theologically, psychologically, and practically. Not all of these problems are negative. There is much intellectual ferment in our time. Talk of "new paradigms," new perceptions emerging from the conversations between theology and science (chaos

2. *New York Times,* 14 November 1995, p. A17. For background to her remarks, see her *Discipleship of Equals* (London: SCM Press, 1993).

theory, cosmology, etc.), new research in the social and biological sciences, postmodernist views of knowledge and language, and the revolution of information technology can cause both excitement and anxiety among the clergy. How does one maintain a firm foundation and ride the whirlwind at the same time? And yet we must do both.

Some people remain in ostrich-like denial about either the possibilities or the malaise. I understand why we clergy resist hearing that we have big challenges and problems. Our own individual situations may be fine. We have plenty to worry about just managing our parishes and pastoring to endless needs. But most clergy will admit that, in the midst of the physical and emotional demands of ordained ministry, the first thing to go is our spiritual life. Indeed, one of the main purposes of "Galilee Moments" is to deal with the need for "routine" spiritual nurture to help ward off truly serious problems. But like it or not, the issues are real for many clergy and for the church, and we cannot ignore them.

The analysis and suggestions in my article have been the focal point of several dozen clergy conferences, retreats, Lenten reading programs, and similar events. Whenever I lead these conferences, two arguments generally come back at me. *"Well, fine, you have analyzed things in ways that touch responsive chords. We will probably agree that some of what you say is right. But two things are missing. First, we really need to articulate a theology of holy orders and the relationship between baptism and ordinations that speaks from the tradition, but in language and insights relevant to today's church* [and some of us are working hard on that].[3] *Second, we also need some help, some practical programs that would in fact aid the clergy to recover that sense of identity, purpose, and mission that, built on the foundation of God's grace, are the heart of our vocation."*

I have felt challenged by that latter request to try to develop a

3. The House of Bishops of the ECUSA, Cornerstone, the Council for the Development of Ministry, the Clergy Leadership Project, the International Anglican Liturgical Consultation, and several other groups have projects underway to articulate a comprehensive theology of baptism and ordination. There is also much discussion occurring about the nature and purpose of each of the historic threefold orders (deacon, presbyter, and bishop); the relationship of the collective priesthood of all believers and individual "ordained selves"; and the definition, theology, and practice of "total ministry." "Galilee Moments" will provide an up-to-date summary and a collection of material from these ongoing discussions.

useful retreat program, in the first instance for the clergy and, in time, for the whole laity as well.[4] This program would be complementary to other clergy wellness initiatives. It would attempt to shore up the intellectual and spiritual foundations of honest, informed, biblical faith, critical respect for the Christian spiritual and ecclesial tradition, and deep theological reflection, all of which must underlie any progress toward long-term spiritual health and provide essential support for spiritually based leadership.

A direction had already been planted in my own spiritual life by Bishop Duncan Gray, Jr., of Mississippi, a wonderful man of principle and grace and the then Chancellor of the University of the South. Bishop Gray had given a fine series of meditations to a seminary "quiet day" on Matthew 28, the very familiar account of our Lord's resurrection reflected in the hymn text quoted above. The women in sadness come to the tomb and discover an angel. The angel tells of the empty tomb; and then the angel says, "Go quickly and tell his disciples, he has been raised from the dead and indeed he is going ahead of you to Galilee, and there you will see him." Shortly after this, the women encounter Jesus and, just in case they had been somewhat stunned when the angel said it, Jesus says again, "Tell my brothers to go back to Galilee, and there they will see me again." Eventually, after worrying about whether somebody had stolen the body, the disciples go back to Galilee as instructed. They encounter Jesus on several epiphanous occasions. The chapter ends with the Great Commission: "All authority in heaven and on earth has been given to me. Go therefore and make disciples of all nations, baptizing them in the name of the Father and of the Son and of the Holy Spirit, and teaching them to obey everything that I have commanded you. And remember, I am with you always, to the end of the age."

Helped by Bishop Gray and a variety of commentaries, I read and reread that chapter with fresh eyes. I began to think about what it was like for the disciples during those three dark days beginning with Good

---

4. I am focusing primarily on clergy spiritual nurture because that is where much of my energy as a seminary dean is right now; but we are hoping that this effort will develop as a program for lay spiritual nurture based on the baptismal covenant and promises, alongside such programs as EFM (Education for Ministry), DOCC (Disciples of Christ in Community), Stephen Ministries, etc.

Friday. Whatever hopes, expectations, ideals, and beliefs they had held had been shattered at the Crucifixion. They had themselves reacted very humanly and very badly — Peter's denial, others running and hiding in fear and despair. I have often thought, when we are experiencing the liturgical glories of the Easter Vigil, when we are hearing all the great stories and collects of Holy Week and Easter Sunday, that the disciples did not have the benefit of all the wonderful prefiguring we get. They did not know on that first Easter morning what the answer was going to be. The more I thought about the disciples, the more I became convinced that, however bleak the situation of the clergy may be at the present time, it could not approach what the disciples had to go through. If it was good advice to them to go back to Galilee and encounter Jesus again, then it is probably good advice for us as well.

In Birmingham, Fleming Rutledge suggested that we draw on the compelling images and metaphors of the Bible to enrich our spiritual understanding. In a brief *lectio divina* excursus, let me focus on one word: *Galilee*. A place name, even one spoken by an angel and repeated by Jesus, may seem somewhat tangential to our ultimate spiritual concerns. But the word has worked powerfully in my imagination, and I hope it will work in yours.

Galilee had always been a special place for Jesus. Tom Wright recently provided in his extraordinary new book some very significant corrections to the scholarship on the religious and social history of the Galilee of Jesus' time.[5] Scripture tells us much about Galilee. It was, of course, the region of Jesus' family home; much of his ministry and his memorable teachings occurred there; it was the land of his most loyal followers — men and women alike; and it was the place where he had called his special companions. It was where he had gone in the aftermath of John the Baptist's arrest, a place of safety and recovery and new beginnings. It was where he first revealed his passion

5. N. T. Wright, *Jesus and the Victory of God* (Minneapolis: Fortress Press, 1996), pp. 37, 40, 158-59, 168, 214. For other references to the literature on Galilee, see the article "Galilee" by Sean Freyne in the *Anchor Bible Dictionary* (New York: Doubleday, 1992) 2: 895-99 and the references there, and two recent books by Richard A. Horsley, *Galilee: History, Politics, People* (Valley Forge, Pa.: Trinity Press, 1995), and *Archaeology, History, and Society in Galilee: The Social Context of Jesus and the Rabbis* (Valley Forge, Pa.: Trinity Press, 1996).

and who he was. It is a place that still calls the Christian imagination by its very sound, as well as its meaning — *Galilee*.

As I was studying the Galilee connection, by sheer happenstance I picked up William Pritchard's memoirs of his life as a student and a teacher of English at Amherst.[6] Early on I came across this paragraph:

> The coming together of words and music in a memorable figure I also experienced in sacred as well as secular tunes. Attending the Episcopal Church as a youth had a lot less to do with concerns of doctrine, salvation, and sin than with rehearsing and singing every week in the junior choir my mother had begun to direct; and playing the organ (only partially since I never learned to use the pedals) for Sunday School services. During the innumerable rehearsals and often at the services themselves, I squirmed with boredom, wishing I were playing basketball or asleep, or just anywhere out of this churchy oppressiveness. But what counted, in the sense that they remain with me today, were the hymns. "Hymns in a Man's Life," D. H. Lawrence called them in his prose reminiscence, and though Lawrence's Non-conformist hymns were not mine, he identified something I also know about. Quoting "a rather banal" hymn that contains the lines "O Galilee, sweet Galilee, where Jesus loved so much to be," Lawrence wrote that, to him, the word *Galilee* had a wonderful special sound. The Lake of Galilee. I don't want to know where it is. I never want to go to Palestine. Galilee is one of those lovely words, not places, that exist in a child's half-formed imagination." He adds that "in my man's imagination, it is just the same."[7]

I was struck by these words, because for similar reasons the word *Galilee* has also had a very powerful impact on me. When I finally went to the Holy Land and actually put my hand in that sea, I felt something very close to a mystical experience. I am sure many of you have felt something like this, too.

Pritchard went on to conclude: "That lovely, glamorous word 'Galilee' existed in and still exists in my imagination because of the hymn that begins: 'Jesus calls us o'er the tumult,' and has a second

---

6. William H. Pritchard, *English Papers: A Teaching Life* (St. Paul, Minn.: Graywolf Press, 1995).

7. Pritchard, *English Papers*, 5-6.

verse that says about this calling 'as of old St. Andrew heard it by the Galilean Lake'."[8] For Pritchard, that lake was a deeply exciting place to hear about. He then borrows a line from Robert Frost to say that such words, such hymns, the images from his religious childhood, remained with him as an adult as "momentary stays against the confusion."[9] That Frost line seems particularly relevant to us because we live in a time when we are surrounded daily by the hectic pace of confusion, and anything that we can hold onto that gives us even partial or momentary stays against confusion is something to be very much cherished.

Jesus called his disciples, on that Easter morning, to go back to Galilee to stay their confusion. There was something meaningful about returning to Galilee where they had first heard his call. They needed more than just some comfort and reassurance; they needed to recover the personal relationship, the sense of call that had first compelled them to leave their fishing boats, to seek out siblings, to abandon lesser tasks for a new vision and a new mission. Jesus said to his disciples, who were at least as confused and depressed, doubting and fearful, as any of us here, "Go back to Galilee where you first met me, and there you will see me again." This was not just some glib Pollyanna-ish "all your problems are over — let's go have a nice day by the seaside." Rather, it was a loving admonition to go back to where they had first heard his words. Perhaps they would hear the call again, hear what it was that led and sustained them to follow Jesus into the proclaimed kingdom of God, with all its trials, tribulations, dangers, and joys.

The significance of this Matthean injunction to go back to Galilee is followed up in Acts 13 in Paul's great sermon in Antioch: "God raised him from the dead, and he appeared to those who came up with him from Galilee who are now his witnesses to the people." A fascinating aspect of this conference is that virtually all the speakers, in their different ways, have said that the greatest evidence for the resurrection is not the empty tomb. The opponents of Jesus were right. Someone could have stolen the body and created a false story. Human beings can be pretty ingenious and devious. It is not the empty

8. Pritchard, *English Papers*, 6.
9. Pritchard, *English Papers*, 6.

tomb that proves anything. It is the appearances of Jesus as resurrected Lord to the women of Galilee, who came to the garden on that Easter morning, and to his disciples, perhaps first on the road to Emmaus or in Jerusalem, but ultimately in Galilee. Sure, Jesus' appearances could have been made up; but, echoing Tom Wright's insights, the fact that we have a record of a group of disciples, male and female, who were willing to live lives witnessing to Jesus and his teachings, often through danger and martyrdom, for the rest of their lives, is very strong evidence that some sort of extraordinary revival took place in those days after the resurrection. Something happened in Galilee between Jesus and his disciples. That is the kind of thing that I want to happen to each of us.

Such reflections are the biblical, theological, and personal inspirations for a new program for the revival of the clergy.[10] Here I can only outline its structure and content very briefly:

"Galilee Moments" will be field-tested at Sewanee and elsewhere during the fall. The initial formal offering will be during the first week of Lent 1998 at Kanuga in North Carolina (March 1-4). The full program is planned as a five-session retreat, which could spread over five days or be condensed into a shorter time span. The format draws on a combination of two great spiritual traditions intrinsically connected to Anglicanism: Benedictine and Wesleyan. They interact very well together and bring out the best in our Catholic and Protestant traditions.

In the first session we will gather together and celebrate the facts of our ministry, our call, our vocation, our priesthood. Gratitude and celebration are extraordinarily important. The great difference between my article on the recovery of priestly identity and Jim Fenhagen's book *Ministry for a New Time*,[11] which have been used together

10. In addition to the writings of N. T. Wright, H. A. Williams, *True Resurrection* (London: Collins, 1972,1983), and Rowan Williams, *Resurrection* (London: Darton, Longman and Todd, 1982), have provided direct and important theological background to "Galilee Moments"; as have, in their different ways, Dietrich Bonhoeffer, *The Cost of Discipleship* (New York: Macmillan, 1949), Henri J. M. Nouwen, *In the Name of Jesus: Reflections on Christian Ministry* (New York: Crossroad, 1992), and Virgilio Elizondo, *Galilean Journey* (Maryknoll, N.Y.: Orbis, 1983).

11. James Fenhagen, *Ministry for a New Time* (Bethesda, Md.: Alban Institute, 1995).

in a number of contexts, is that my piece is much grumpier than his. I received a letter from a seminary professor friend thanking me for a "splendidly cranky essay."[12] Fenhagen's book stresses, much more than I do in my article, the importance of *gratitude* as foundational to our revival. I have told Jim that he is able to be grateful because he is now a *retired* seminary dean; one still in the trenches has little time for gratitude. But I acknowledge and incorporate his good and significant insight, and I want to celebrate at the beginning of the retreat, with great gratitude, what God has given to those of us called into the ordained ministries.

After a time of gratitude, we will work, with trained facilitators, at forming the small "Galilee groups" that are crucial for this kind of retreat. Such groups, emerging from our shared identities, experiences, and hopes, are meant to be safe places where trust can blossom, where honesty, openness, challenge, and support can lead to deeper spiritual selves and new spiritual friendships.

In this context, we can look first at the life of St. Peter and then at the frustrations, sins, mistakes, and failures whose scars all of us clergy inevitably bear. We will examine the idea that "burn-out" is not a disabling condition, but rather a cycle imaged in 2 Timothy 4:1-8 as pouring ourselves out as a libation and then needing to refill our buckets over and over again. We can recognize "tiredness" as a condition to be honored — as honest workers, good athletes, and mothers all know.

We will end this opening process with a Eucharist in which we will, as John Claypool says in his "offertory altar calls," try to lay our past baggage, our pain, whatever obstacles we have, on the altar. Then, I hope, we will go to a time of quiet and rest, maybe even a tired and peaceful sleep, having truly given both our thanks and most of our "bad stuff" to God and begun new relationships which may become lifelong sources of joy and support.

During the second session (or day) we will focus on recalling our first sense of ourselves as Christians and our understanding of our vocations as "ordained selves." Here retreatants will establish, and begin to draw on, the first of their "Galilee moments." This "moment" will recall one of their most significant early encounters with

12. Personal communication from the Rev. Professor Owen Thomas.

Jesus — a conversion experience, a sense of call, a feeling of new birth. This "Galilee moment" can have been in the form of a "Damascus Road experience" or it can have been something that developed gradually; but I want people to pursue a very precise and vivid remembering of what it was that drew them to their vocation, to following Jesus in the first place. As with later "Galilee moments," this will provide a defining occasion to which one can return again and again to use as a wellspring of spiritual identity and strength.

The third session/day will focus on the truly formative narratives and stories that define us as Christians, individually and in community. A series of meditations, Bible studies, and discussions will recall the content of Jesus' life, relationships, teachings, and actions, and relate them to our lives and ministries. These gospel exercises are practical versions of what Tom Wright called us to in his lecture — that intense encounter with the real Jesus who is revealed to us, whom we can discover by study, and to whom we can bond in a special way in our spiritual life.[13]

The fourth session/day will consider both the baptismal and the ordination vows that we have taken. A series of theological and personal meditations, especially on those vows in which we are called to align our wills with the will of Christ, align our minds with the mind of Christ, align our lives with the life of Christ as models for others, will express the meaning we attach to these vows that give shape to our lives. For many, this will likely be both the intellectual and the emotional climax of the retreat, although nothing in the content or process will manipulate or "require" an emotional response. After a time of personal reflection and prayer, we will reach a point where, in another "Galilee moment," we recall our ordination and say a confident and humble "yes" once again. Or we will begin to ask

13. While my understanding of Jesus in "Galilee Moments" is influenced by the scholarship of Dean N. T. Wright, several people have commented on the echo of one of Marcus J. Borg's books, or at least its title, *Meeting Jesus Again for the First Time* (San Francisco: HarperCollins, 1994). I, like Tom Wright (*Jesus and the Victory of God*, pp. 75ff., especially p. 78), find Borg the most sympathetic of the people associated with the Jesus Seminar, and I have always enjoyed my encounters with him. That does not mean that I agree with him. I see "Galilee Moments" as both an extension of some of his opinions and a challenge/answer to others. The "Galilee Moments" presentations will consider and respond to contemporary scholarship on Jesus.

honest, painful, but perhaps liberating questions about a particular vocation that once was compelling, but is no more. The intensely personal and private nature of these thoughts will be strictly respected, but the retreat will also have experienced chaplains available if any participants want or need to talk.

One of the significant findings of many wellness initiatives, according to representatives of the Church Pension Fund and others, is that perhaps 20 percent of the clergy still active in the cure of souls either should not continue or would like not to continue their lives as priests. But there is virtually no way to "get out" with honor. For many, resigning one's orders implies failure — spiritual or personal — and suspicion that we embezzled something, that we drink too much, or, most likely, that we have been tainted by some sexual misconduct. While I still wrestle with the theology of the indelibility of orders and related issues, I think we must find a way in the church for people honestly to say, "Whatever was right for me and for the church once is no longer where I feel God wants me to be." And sometimes the church must have the courage to say something like this to ordained persons who cannot see it or say it themselves. Neither decision is easy; but we clergy and the church must face the issue.

This fourth session/day also marks the chance to move beyond an individualistic focus and to make both a recommitment and a reconciliation to the institutional church that has been both our mother and sometimes our terror. Many ordained people today are so alienated from the institutional church and from other clergy that they exist in a state of rage and of spiritual and functional paralysis. In a context of anger and insecurity, little, if any, "mutual ministry" or sharing of power with others (clergy or laity) is possible. Antagonism and lack of trust blight the lives of individuals and the church.

We hope that the content of the fourth session/day will answer three potential criticisms of the premises and structure of the "Galilee Moments" retreat program: that it is too individualistic, too "clericalist," and perhaps semi-Pelagian (a charge Anglicanism has often faced). I do believe in the call and ordination of individuals and the concept of "ordained selves."[14] Of course, I affirm Terry Holmes's

---

14. See n. 1 above, and such biblical references as Jeremiah 1:4 and Galatians 1:15.

portrayal of the "priest in community."[15] That relationship is rightly a given in today's ecclesiology, although I think Holmes's real message about priestly identity is widely misunderstood. I believe strongly in the *collegium* of each order and in the "priesthood of all believers." But I have serious doubts, theologically and practically, about some current ideas that *all* priesthood is "collective," that there is no *personal* priestly (or, presumably, diaconal or episcopal) identity. By its teaching and by its process, "Galilee Moments" will try to offer a balance between corporate and individual emphases. "Galilee Moments" does not envision or encourage a new "clericalism"; in fact, just the opposite. It will stress that "identity" is not about "status." It will emphasize an inner strength and peace that fosters true humility. It will define the clergy as honest workers, striving — with all other Christians — not for our own glory, but for the glory of God. As for semi-Pelagianism, we will preach, in every possible way, the essential grace of God in all good that we do; but we also believe in the responsibility of the individual — *iustus et peccator* — as, in Hooker's understanding, a free-will participant in the purposes of God and the upbuilding of the church.[16]

Finally, in the fifth session/day, we will look forward. A mistake I made at the beginning of my design was structuring almost the whole retreat "looking back." As a historian by training and profession, perhaps I live too much in the rearview mirror. I discovered as I talked to clergy conferences and elsewhere that many people thought it was indeed helpful to go back to original conversion experiences, or to their original calls to the priesthood, or to ordination services and vows; but going back was not enough. The important thing is (Bishop Gray had said this, and finally I heard it) that Matthew 28 does not stop with going back to Galilee. Jesus took the disciples back to Galilee in order to enable and strengthen them to go out as witnesses and servants to the entire world. So we, too, will end by looking forward with excitement to working in new vineyards vastly different from the ones many of us grew up in; to a revived sense of prophecy, service, and evangelism in a radically altered social and cultural milieu; to the

---

15. U. T. Holmes, *The Priest in Community* (New York: Seabury, 1978).

16. John E. Booty, "Richard Hooker," in William J. Wolf (ed.), *The Spirit of Anglicanism* (Wilton, Conn.: Morehouse-Barlow, 1979), especially pp. 17ff.

fruits of our call and labor in God's grace; to our necessary place in gathering, building, inspiring, and reconciling a eucharistic community of faith for the church and the world.

In this time of an ideologically polarized church, "Galilee Moments" is neither "liberal" nor "conservative." It is not even "centrist." Rather, it means to be *radical* in the literal sense of trying to reach and nurture the life-giving *roots* of Christianity. In an image that Alan Jones and I have both used, our spiritual journeys can be like constructing a beautiful cathedral spire, soaring upward, pointing our hearts and minds toward God; but we can build it only as strong and tall as the buried, unseen foundations will support. "Galilee Moments" will tend to our roots, shore up our foundations. With strong common roots, the church can be a healthy and persevering oak, whose sturdy trunk is able to sustain continuous new and beautiful growth — and even those shaky limbs that some of us occasionally choose to crawl out on.

Earlier I said that the spiritual context of "Galilee Moments" drew on both our Benedictine and Wesleyan heritages. There will be teaching, talking, praying, common worship, silence, and private time for reflection, relaxation, and recommitment — time to be open to the voice and grace of our Lord. There will also be hymn singing, which John and Charles Wesley thought, and I still think, crucial to our spiritual health. I hark back to what William Pritchard and D. H. Lawrence wrote about the importance of hymn texts and tunes in nurturing our imaginations.

Sometime in the future, we hope to establish a physical and spiritual home in Galilee itself, where people will go for followup retreats, Bible study, and a sense of Christian community. We hope that, even sooner, diocesan "Galilee groups" will be formed, with the support and participation of bishops, to be safe places of trust, honesty, and spiritual support for both new and established clergy. We dream big dreams, but not impossible ones, of a revitalized clergy to work with a revitalized laity in the church's holy mission in and to this world.

"Galilee Moments" is largely about recovering the *passion* — both the passion of Jesus Christ and our own passion for the vocation we have been called, equipped, and ordained to follow. As I was working on these plans, a priest said something to me that I will never forget. He said, "You can try all the gimmicks, you can do all the 'processes' in the world. I said yes to this vocation because I wanted to follow Jesus. Somewhere along the line I lost Jesus, and I need to get him back." "Galilee Moments" intends to help people find that which is already in them, to reclaim the stories, the call, the expectations, the hopes that by God's grace are there, and to find in those gifts not only something that will sustain us in our individual spiritual lives, but also something that will provide a font of living water out of which we can preach and proclaim Jesus Christ to others who hunger and thirst for truth and redemption, for lives in the service of peace and justice, for hope in the promise of the Resurrection.

We clergy must find some way to recover the passion that only the personal presence and inspiration of Jesus in our lives can provide. I do not mean to denigrate in any way what other clergy leadership and clergy wellness projects are trying to do. I pray to God that we clergy and the church body as a whole are all getting healthier because of this work. But Sewanee is going to try to do something just a little bit different, something that aspires to be both as sophisticated as the latest biblical and theological scholarship and as honest as a child's first faith. We will call clergy to retreats in which the real historical Jesus and our relationship with Jesus are focal points that can be reclaimed and can provide, to repeat our basic image, the *wellspring* of truth and hope to sustain us and our ministries in an ever more secular and complex world. As it was for his earliest followers, may it so be for us.

Let me close with a foretaste of our time in retreat together by offering four deeply moving hymns to sing alone or with others and to use as classic texts for reflection. The first evokes the haunting link between ultimate sacrifice and ultimate peace:

> They cast their nets in Galilee
> just off the hills of brown;
> such happy, simple fisher folk,
> before the Lord came down.
>
> Contented, peaceful fishermen,
> before they ever knew
> the peace of God that filled their hearts
> brimful, and broke them too.

Young John who trimmed the flapping sail,
homeless, in Patmos died.
Peter, who hauled the teeming net,
head down was crucified.

The peace of God, it is no peace,
but strife closed in the sod.
Yet let us pray for but one thing —
the marvelous peace of God.   (Hymn 661, *Hymnal 1982*)

The second, a complex text and tune, recalls the role of holy Galilean
women in the life and resurrection of the Lord:

The first one ever, oh, ever to know
of the birth of Jesus, was the Maid Mary,
was Mary the Maid of Galilee,
and blessed is she, is she who believes.
Oh, blessed is she who believes in the Lord,
oh, blessed is she who believes.
She was Mary the Maid of Galilee,
and blessed is she, is she who believes.

The first one ever, oh, ever to know
of Messiah, Jesus, when he said, "I am he,"
was the Samaritan woman who drew from the well,
and blessed is she, is she who perceives.
Oh, blessed is she who perceives the Lord,
oh, blessed is she who perceives.
'Twas the Samaritan woman who drew from the well,
and blessed is she, is she who perceives.

The first ones ever, oh, ever to know
of the rising of Jesus, his glory to be,
were Mary, Joanna, and Magdalene,
and blessed are they, are they who see.
Oh, blessed are they who see the Lord,
oh, blessed are they who see.
They were Mary, Joanna, and Magdalene,
and blessed are they, are they who see.
                    (Hymn 673, *Hymnal 1982*)

The third, consistently voted the most beloved hymn in the Anglican Communion, with a text drawn from the brokenness and yearning of lives caught in addiction, comes close to stating the hopes of the "Galilee Moments" program:

> Dear Lord and Father of mankind,
> forgive our foolish ways!
> Reclothe us in our rightful mind,
> in purer lives thy service find,
> in deeper reverence, praise,
> in deeper reverence, praise.
>
> In simple trust like theirs who heard,
> beside the Syrian sea,
> the gracious calling of the Lord,
> let us, like them, without a word,
> rise up and follow thee,
> rise up and follow thee.
>
> O Sabbath rest by Galilee!
> O calm of hills above,
> where Jesus knelt to share with thee
> the silence of eternity
> interpreted by love!
> interpreted by love!
>
> Drop thy still dews of quietness,
> till all our strivings cease;
> take from our souls the strain and stress,
> and let our ordered lives confess
> the beauty of thy peace,
> the beauty of thy peace.
>
> Breathe through the heats of our desire
> thy coolness and thy balm;
> let sense be dumb, let flesh retire;
> speak through the earthquake, wind, and fire,
> O still, small voice of calm,
> O still, small voice of calm.   (Hymn 653, *Hymnal 1982*)

And, finally, Hymn 550, although I suspect most of you will mentally hum it to its more popular tune, entitled unsurprisingly

"Galilee." (If you don't remember how it goes, see almost any Protestant hymnal published before 1980.)

> Jesus calls us; o'er the tumult
> of our life's wild, restless sea,
> day by day his clear voice soundeth,
> saying, "Christian, follow me";
>
> as, of old, Saint Andrew heard it
> by the Galilean lake,
> turned from home and toil and kindred,
> leaving all for his dear sake.
>
> Jesus calls us from the worship
> of the vain world's golden store;
> from each idol that would keep us,
> saying, "Christian, love me more."
>
> In our joys and in our sorrows,
> days of toil and hours of ease,
> still he calls, in cares and pleasures,
> "Christian, love me more than these."
>
> Jesus calls us! By thy mercies,
> Savior, may we hear thy call,
> give our hearts to thine obedience,
> serve and love thee best of all.

As we all seek to make the truth about Jesus the foundation of our minds, hearts, wills, and lives, I look forward to developing our "Galilee Moments" together sometime soon.[17]

17. I am very grateful to the many people who responded helpfully to earlier versions of this paper/talk. I particularly thank Maria Campbell (Trinity, Wall Street) for her close reading, many very insightful suggestions, and strong encouragement. For special help in producing this version, I thank Dr. James Dunkly and my office staff. I also thank my colleagues on the Senior Staff of the School of Theology Programs Center who have played a crucial and ongoing role in the development of "Galilee Moments."

*   *   *

For more information about "Galilee Moments," write:

"Galilee Moments"
School of Theology Programs Center
University of the South
335 Tennessee Avenue
Sewanee TN 37383-0001
or e-mail
theology@sewanee.edu

Jesus and Human Experience

DIOGENES ALLEN

I HAVE BEEN ASKED as a philosopher to talk about human experience and Jesus. A philosopher who is a Christian is concerned to understand Jesus in the large context of human knowledge and the human search for wisdom, so that we may understand Jesus better and learn how to see all things in the light of God.

The very title of this address poses a serious question. For many intellectuals today the notion of "human experience" is problematic. They reject the Enlightenment's assumption that there are universal values and universal meanings. Each culture has its own values and outlook. Christianity is seen as a mere cultural product. In addition, some have said that Christianity is so gender-loaded and so patriarchal as to need a thorough turning inside out, if not outright rejection. In short, people do not share the same experiences, conditions, or aspirations. How then can Jesus be seen to be relevant to human experience, and thereby have universal significance, if in fact there is no such thing as common human experience?

My approach to the topic is to recognize that people in different times and places are indeed different. People are hardly uniform in a single society, and much less so in the world at large. But I think the notion of "human experience" has some meaning. I take it to mean that life is like a journey for everyone. All of us have to grow physically to reach adulthood. We also have to grow socially. We face questions about what we can become, what we ought to become, what we can hope for. This is true of all of us. In our journey through life, some of what we encounter is pretty common. All of us encounter power and subordination. All of us seek a place in the order around us. People in all societies and strata of society need restoration and renewal. We encounter evil and all of us are liable to suffering and great loss, as well as aging and death. Aspiration for righteousness or purity is common, and there is a powerful desire for significance and to be significant. These matters are not restricted to one race, one sex, one society, or one stratum of a society. Let me now turn from these abstractions and look at these matters more concretely.

I. Our Journey and Place in the Order

Not long ago I heard a short story read aloud. Virtually every word seemed to grip the audience. Afterwards I wondered why. It was not simply because it was a good story and had been read with great artistry. Rather, it was because as the audience heard the story unfold, it did not know which part of it would be important. For a man actually to come out of a house, get into a car, and slowly drive away is a prosaic event. But when it is part of a story, it can hold an audience's attention because it just might turn out to be significant.

In a well-constructed short story everything makes a contribution to the overall effect, just as every part of a great painting does. But everything in actual life is not experienced as making a contribution. Only some of our life is interesting. As our life unfolds, most of it is utterly dull. Well-constructed stories appeal to us because all the events make a contribution to the whole. Tacitly, perhaps, we wish that all the events in our lives were interesting or at least contributed to some overall meaning.

In *Orthodoxy*, G. K. Chesterton described how he eventually came to the conviction that life was indeed like a story. In fact, it was similar to an adventure story. In an adventure story, there is some important goal that requires dedication if it is to be achieved. The valor of loyal companions, who have faced danger and endured losses, is prized. Chesterton showed that these and other features are present in Christianity's understanding of life, and how Christianity's understanding of life gave shape and direction to his own.

Chesterton discovered for himself what today is widely called "the narrative form of human life." We quite naturally express who we are in the form of a story about ourselves. We introduce ourselves to other people by telling them where we are from, where we were educated, who we know, whether we are married and have a family, tell them about our goals, and the like. Our identity is gained through time, and cannot be expressed apart from an account of our specific passage through time.

The notion of the narrative form of life is used today in biblical and theological studies as well as in philosophy and ethics. Less high-flown, it finds its way into literature. Consider the novel *Hawaii,* by James Michener. Michener describes the early missionaries' surprise at the interest shown by the native Polynesians in the genealogy of Jesus. That Abraham was the father of Isaac, and Isaac the father of Jacob, and Jacob the father of Judah, and Judah the father of Perez, and so on is perhaps the dullest part of the Bible. If one seeks to engage the interest of most readers today, Matthew's opening is certainly not a model to emulate. Why then did the Polynesians listen to it again and again with such interest? They had a genealogy of their own people, which traced them through the centuries and specified their own place in the sequence of time and place. It enabled them in effect to say, we are here because there was a "before" that we can trace back from where we now are. They were rooted, rather than lost in the stars and surrounding sea. There was an order, and they had a place in the order. It transcended the individual and gave every individual a place. In addition, the stories associated with each name in their genealogy gave them guidance for their own lives, and the strength and confidence to face the future. They could be inspired to go forward because of all that they had been through as a people.

Because they had an essential interest in their place in the order, they listened with great interest to the genealogy of Jesus, to the stories associated with the various generations, and especially to Jesus' life. They soon incorporated their own history into the larger Christian order because it completed the understanding they derived from their own history.

Genealogy does not play an important part in most people's lives, nor is it necessary that it should. But it is important that we should have an interest in finding our place in a larger order. Without that interest most of the Bible is boring. The biblical past is not *our* past in the sense of giving our lives a "fix" in time and space. We are unable to draw upon that past, which is permeated with that which comes "from above," for guidance, strength, and hope. We are not part of what is larger and greater than ourselves. To the extent that we are interested only in ourselves, our present is a fleeting present, rather than one connected to what has gone before and directed toward a hopeful future. We become only a fleeting and narrow piece of consciousness, unaware of so much that is real and valuable.

Consider a story told by a teacher, who made a tour of England because of his interest in change bell-ringing. Change bell-ringing is an English style of ringing a series of very large bells according to highly intricate sequences. Each bell has a single ringer, who must pull a bell-rope at precisely the right instant to fit into the sequence. The results of this physically and mentally demanding cooperative effort are far more beautiful than any individual could produce alone. It is musically much more accomplished than the simple tunes played by carillon bells.

On the train to the airport at the end of his tour the teacher was disturbed by a couple of teenagers, who had been to Europe for the summer. They were not only being loud and obnoxious, squirting sodas at each other, but they were utterly unaware of the lovely and historic countryside through which the train was passing. As a teacher, he was deeply concerned that they did not even realize what they were missing. Perhaps because of his recent experience of bell-ringing, he asked himself, "How will they find their place in the order?"

Change bell-ringing is a parable of life. It requires the acceptance and subordination of oneself to an order. So, too, does every other worthwhile activity. Participation in an order, whether through the scientific study of the natural world, taking part in community life, or the creation and appreciation of art, can point one to the ultimate source of all freedom and order.

To find our place in the proximate order, much less the ultimate order, is not always easy. But some have even ceased to try. As Walker Percy, the late novelist, once said in conversation, "I have learned that the most important difference between people is between those for whom life is a quest and those for whom it is not." A quest involves asking ourselves questions about what is worth doing, having, and being. We often set these questions aside because we are afraid that we cannot determine what we are, what we ought to be, and what we may hope for.

Günther Grass, the well-known German novelist and poet, portrays what it is like to be a person who has ceased to search for a significant and meaningful life. (My translation of his poem "Hearsay" is literal.)

> With my ear have I today
> four times the fire siren heard.
> I sit at the table with my ear
> and say:
> Once again the fire siren.
>
> I could just as well have said:
> The huge consumption of paper bags.
> Or:
> The shoes must be taken to the cobbler.
> Or:
> Tomorrow is Saturday.
> However, I said:
> Once again the fire siren.
> Still, whoever correctly understands me,
> knows,
> that with the consumption of paper bags,
> the taking of shoes to the cobbler,
> by Saturday, I meant,
> the weekend.

Whoever correctly understands me, says the poet, understands that nothing in this person's life makes sense or has any value. The items he mentions — buying things that consume lots of paper bags, shoes that must be taken to the cobbler, or the fact that tomorrow is Saturday — do not connect or hold together. They are just one time after another. They add up to nothing; they are completely interchangeable. The insignificance of life is evident from the fact that the person hears fire alarms — hears them four times — and is utterly unmoved. The fire trucks that are heard going by are no different from getting shoes repaired or going shopping. It does not matter that fires cause damage, irretrievable losses, death, and grief. Just as the weekend is detached from the activities of the week, so too is the person in the poem detached and uninvolved because there is finally nothing worthwhile to care for, to struggle for, to suffer for, to rejoice in, to hope for. The lack of anything worthwhile lies behind the poem's air of unreality. Life is hearsay because it is indirect, not direct, and it is hearsay because the person in the poem is utterly passive — things just happen.

A person who is not on a journey, searching for what is worth becoming, is a person who, like the person in the poem, has lost his or her life. It ceases to be a life worth living. Only vegetative needs and instinctual impulses keep such a person alive.

The price of being without any vision of a goal for life is therefore very high. In Muriel Spark's novel *The Prime of Miss Jean Brodie,* an inspiring teacher lifts a group of school girls out of their dreary, daily grind with her buoyant spirit and refrain, "Without a vision the people perish." For a time, this Old Testament quotation was glibly tossed off at chic cocktail parties, without its ultimate biblical source or even its proximate source being known. People also frequently failed to realize that the vision Jean Brodie had in mind was Mussolini's. Without a vision people perish, but they also perish with the wrong vision. We need not just any purpose but one that leads us into truth. Where is that to be found? How is that to be found? By being restored.

II. A Comparison of Jesus and Socrates

Consider, for example, Mary Magdalene, one of Jesus' followers. Mary was a notorious person, an easy lay, as we might put it today. No one had any respect for her. However much our mores have changed, it isn't hard for us to recognize that there is a very real difference between people of either sex who are grossly promiscuous and those who are not. What amazed people was Jesus' power to transform Mary into a wholesome person whom everyone could respect. Part of Jesus' greatness was his effect on her life, which was there for everyone to see.

In recent years biblical commentators have pointed out that, even though Mary Magdalene had been regarded throughout Christian history as a prostitute, the biblical texts that refer to her do not explicitly state this. Whether she was or not, the point still stands: Whatever had been wrong with her, Jesus put it right, and people were amazed. Probably one reason she is so often mentioned by those who were with Jesus during his ministry is to call attention to what Jesus could do. It is as if the various texts were saying: "See what this man can do!" But to appreciate more fully the greatness of Jesus' power, we may contrast it to that of Socrates.

In *The Symposium* Socrates and some friends were discussing the nature of love when Alcibiades, one of Socrates' former pupils, barged into the dining room drunk as a lord. Alcibiades had been Socrates' most promising disciple — clever, handsome, well connected. Now he was leading a life of dissipation. The setting of the dialogue is a flashback, so its readers know that soon after this meeting with Socrates, Alcibiades betrayed his country and, even worse, revealed the secrets of one of the mystery religions, which was considered to be the most despicable thing a person could do.

In the dialogue, Alcibiades lavishly praised Socrates, and explained how he had become Socrates' pupil or disciple. He said that he really could not explain Socrates' attraction. Socrates was not good looking and he spoke in the everyday language of the marketplace (somewhat as Jesus did) rather than with the impressive rhetoric of the famous teachers of the day. Yet, he admitted that somehow Socrates' words got into you. You could feel them swell like seeds that are starting to grow, and they made him feel ashamed of the way he lived. But it becomes clear in the dialogue that nonetheless Alcibiades was unable to change, and that however much Socrates cared for him and he for Socrates, Alcibiades was now beyond help because he had become corrupt. He was beyond the power even of Socrates' great wisdom and love.

People in ancient times feared corruption. Just as food can become spoiled so that it cannot be restored to wholesomeness, so, too, can people become so corrupt as to be beyond restoration. This is why Socrates, Plato, and Aristotle, the greatest philosophers of ancient times, feared easy pleasures. Children were carefully supervised because if left wholly to their own devices they would do whatever was fun. Easy pleasures that did not develop character and self-discipline, were contrasted with higher pleasures that came only after the demanding effort of learning how to read or to play an instrument. Unless one has developed self-discipline, easy pleasures become addictive — the more you have, the more you want. When it is a choice between making an effort and an easy pleasure, the easy pleasure frequently wins. A person who follows this course finds that in time boredom becomes more and more insistent, and eventually erodes all self-restraint. In time all sense of propriety, and even the ability to direct one's own life, is lost. Then one is unable to change without a great deal of help. Some people, like Alcibiades and Mary Magdalene, reach the point where no one can help them. It was said that Jesus cast seven demons out of Mary Magdalene. This indicates the completeness of her corruption (Luke 8:2; Mark 16:9).[1]

In the *Symposium,* Plato publicly admitted that Alcibiades had gone beyond the reach of the restorative power of Socrates, the person Plato most admired. In the New Testament, Jesus is portrayed as able to restore to wholesomeness those who had become corrupt. His parable of the Prodigal Son, who was restored to a place of honor by his father's power and love, was not just a story; it described something that Jesus himself could do, and something that people could see that he had done in the case of Mary Magdalene. She was a concrete reason for people to listen to him and to follow him. What Jesus did is not only beyond the power of the greatest philosophers, it was beyond the power of the greatest teachers of the Jewish Law. One of today's popular fallacies, which has only recently been dented, is that a really good psychiatrist has the knowledge and power to restore anyone to a normal, productive life, no matter what that person has done and no matter what he or she has become. But those in the practice of psychiatric medicine know only too well that a great deal is beyond their reach, just as a great deal is beyond the reach of nonpsychiatric medicine.[2]

III. Hegel's Master-Slave Relation Compared to Jesus' Relation to His Followers

The power to restore people who have become corrupt leads us to the general theme of power in human experience. Today it is com-

---

1. In ancient Israel seven implied totality, fullness, or wholeness. This is evident in the opening of Genesis where it is said that God created the heavens and the earth in seven days.

In the case of demonic possession, seven signifies total, complete, or maximal possession. See *Theological Dictionary of the New Testament,* ed. Gerhard Kittel, trans. G. W. Bromiley (Grand Rapids: Eerdmans, 1978), 2:628, 630-31.

2. See, for example, M. O'C. Drury, *The Danger of Words* (London: Routledge and Kegan Paul, 1973).

monly said, especially by those who endorse a postmodernist creed, that all values and meaning are human or cultural projections, so that all social hierarchy is based on domination by the most powerful groups in various societies. This claim is also made about religious institutions and teachings.

At the core of the Christian life is the fact that people have a Lord, someone to whom they belong and to whom they are obedient. How can people be free if they have a master? How can people be free if they have someone to obey?

Jean-Paul Sartre, like so many in the present culture who want to be in control of their own lives, claimed that the two notions — freedom and God — contradict each other. To be human is to be free, to be autonomous. So the very idea of God reduces people to slavery, and is essentially antihuman.

You do not need to endorse Sartre's claim to recognize the resentment we would feel at having a boss, a ruler, or anyone else telling us what to do all the time. How would that be human fulfillment? How could that be self-fulfillment? How could that be happiness? The Christian gospel claims that the spiritual life is to be one of fullness of life and blessedness. How can that develop from a relationship to one who has unquestionable authority over us, especially if we think that blessedness includes a significant degree of self-direction? So the spiritual life has at its center the question, How can we be free when we are ruled by a master?

I will deal with this question by examining Hegel's analysis of the relation between master and slave in his *Phenomenology*, in which he exhibits the principles that govern the relation. Then I will see if they are present in Jesus' treatment of his disciples.

Hegel tells us that in human life there is conflict, with each person seeking to get his or her own way. One resolution of the conflict is the master-slave relation. One person dominates the other completely. From the point of view of one of the people — the master — this is the optimal resolution; for that person's will is obeyed and hence his personhood is fully realized.

But there is an irony in the situation. The master cannot be truly independent or free. To assert his independence, his mastery, he must have something that is not himself. He must have something to pay him deference, something to subordinate. He has status as master only as long as he has a slave. Thus he does not have perfect independence.

The master tries to keep this truth hidden, to suppress it, by making his control more and more arbitrary, so there is no recourse beyond his will as to how he treats the slave. The more arbitrary his control, the stronger the slave's dependence, and hence the greater his sense of independence. But clearly it is self-defeating; for this consciousness of independence requires the existence of something to subordinate and something that can recognize the master's dominance.

Another feature of the master-slave relation is the master's contempt for the slave. By becoming subservient to him, the slave is debased and so is odious. The slave is debased and odious because he really is a person, just like the master. They are essentially the same. Were the slave not a person, there would be no contempt. Why be contemptuous of a river that yields to a dam? Nor do we hold dogs in contempt because they obey us. To call a person a "dog" shows that we have contempt for such obedience when it is exhibited by a person. So the master's very contempt is an implicit recognition that the slave is a person, and that the relation is an improper one.

The relation is also marked by resentment. The master resents the slave because he needs him to have the status of a master. The slave resents the master because he must obey him. Finally, there is envy. The slave wishes that he had power like the master. He envies and secretly admires what the master can do, and wants to do it as well. He wants to be a master himself.

IV. The Relation of Jesus and His Disciples

It is very clear in the four gospel accounts that the relation of Jesus to his disciples, though one of dominance and subordination, is very different from the one Hegel describes. Jesus does not gain or hold subordinates by force. He calls disciples, so that there is an element of choice on their part in becoming subordinate to him. He seeks to confer benefits on them by teaching them. He even performs an act of a servant when he washes their feet. We perceive no resentment nor contempt in his treatment of his disciples. Why is this so? What enables Jesus to be a different kind of lord?

Let us approach this by looking at a relation I live with all the time: that of teacher to students. In this relation teachers are in the role of superiors. Within certain limits, we tell our students what to do. What keeps this relation from being that of a Hegelian master with slaves? How can we be the boss and the students not feel or be degraded, or feel resentful? How can we operate on the basis of being boss and not feel contempt for students as underlings?

The relation of superior-subordinate is justified if there are genuine grounds for one to be dominant and the other to be subordinate. If there is some basis for the teacher to command, to lead, and for the student to follow, then there is no violation of personality.

In teaching one ground of justification is that a teacher knows something the pupil does not know. The teacher has some skills, some means of getting answers, and some experience which the pupil lacks. The relation is thus based on a difference. But this is not enough to justify the relation of superior and subordinate. The goal of the teacher must be to enable the pupil to became independent of the teacher. The pupil must eventually be able to learn without the teacher. Many of us teach in such a way that the pupil is dependent on lecture notes, and never masters the principles and skills of a field. Some teachers not only fail to do these things, but some even take a secret delight in their pupils remaining dependent, in remaining essentially inferior to themselves forever.

Each type of relation differs. Doctor-patient, lawyer-client, pastor-congregation, parent-child. Each needs to be looked at in terms of its own particularity. One cannot simply transfer what is true of the teacher-pupil relation to others, or vice versa. There may be similarities; there may be great differences. I only want to make one point with the teacher-pupil example: For a relation of superior and subordinate to be different from Hegel's master-slave relation, there must be some genuine basis for the two roles. There is none in Hegel's; there is only brute, raw power.

Now what is the basis of Jesus' lordship? On what does it rest, so that he can indeed be our Lord, can command us, have us depend on him always, without this being destructive of our personality? What makes him a different kind of lord than Hegel's master?

The foundation of Jesus' relation to his disciples and to us is that he does not need us. This may sound harsh and false at first, but it is really the basis of his ability to serve us and elevate us. He does not need us in this sense. Jesus is Lord because of who he is, not because he has followers. He is Lord by his own inherent reality. He is Lord because he is the Son of God. It isn't because of us that he is the Son of God. Hegel's master is a master only if he has slaves. His *status* depends on having subordinates. He cannot afford to serve them; for then he ceases to be master. He cannot afford to have them come to any sense of fullness; for any degree of independence threatens his status.

But Jesus is the Son of the Father whether we like it or not. His position, his status, his authority does not spring from anything human. It does not depend even on our acknowledgment. He is Son of God without a single disciple.

Precisely because he does not need us, precisely because his status does not rest on us, he can serve us. He can wash his disciples' feet, and not thereby cease to be the Son. He can free people of demons and from other ailments, and this improvement in their condition does not threaten his status. He can be free to let people choose voluntarily to respond to his call to follow him; for whether they reject or accept him, he is still the Son of the Father. He can even be slain for us, bearing the awful catastrophe of human evil, without ceasing to be Lord. Precisely because he differs from us in kind, his lordship does not need to reduce our reality. Because his lordship rests on the Father, he is free to enhance us.

Because Hegel's master does not really differ in kind from his slaves, since both are equally creatures, his lordship is destructive. Hegel's master must deny the personality of his slaves. He must seek to absorb their reality by making them an extension of his will: "Do this, do that. Give me the product of your labor." He does everything for his own sake, in order to be a lord, in order to have the status of a master.

How different orders and commands are when they are from one that does not seek to deny our person, but to enhance it. By his commands and authority Jesus does not seek to deny our person, but to free us. He seeks to free us of the need to have our person established by domination over others. He seeks to free us of the need to gain recognition at the expense of others. The basis of our freedom is that he gives us our status as people destined to share in the life of God, now and always. That is who we are; that is what we are: creatures destined for an eternal happiness. That status is conferred on us. It is not a gift of this world; for it cannot be grasped by an employment of all our talent, ingenuity, strength, or wit. It cannot be attained by gaining prestige, power, or status over others. We therefore do not have to compete with each other in order to become ourselves; for what we are to become is not to be gained in the realm of earthly dominance, founded on the standards of earthly success. We can be free precisely because he is free. His lordship is not based on anything earthly. So he can serve us. It is by following him that we can enter the kingdom in which we can serve each other.

V. Facing Power in Such a Way That What Is at Stake Is Not Lost

Another aspect of the theme of power is brought out by a look at the way Jesus met his death at the hands of those with authority. In the face of a threat to public order, those with public power and the responsibility for maintaining public peace, even if they care about justice, as Pilate did, are sometimes under pressure to sacrifice justice — and with it, all pretense of determining whose views are correct when it comes to life's big questions. In spite of the faith of the eighteenth- and nineteenth-century political reformers, such as Voltaire and Marx, in the "verdict of history," the arena of political decisions is not likely to be a place where the big issues of life are discussed or decided solely or even primarily on the basis of truth and justice.

So when Pilate washed his hands in public to indicate his personal disagreement with the charges against Jesus, he made it clear that the truth of the matter in the controversy between Jesus and his adversaries had not been settled. His enemies succeeded in having Jesus condemned to death, but Pilate indicated that what they were doing was unjust and did not settle the matter of who was right. Ironically, Pilate, who had tried to get around the controversy by letting Jesus go, is the one who ordered his execution. But at least he made it clear that Jesus was executed, not for political sedition, but because of what he claimed to be. In spite of the sentence passed on Jesus and his execution, the question still remained, Is what Jesus claimed true? Pilate, who was not a Jew and something of a cynic, as evidenced by his rhetorical question, What is Truth?, nonetheless allowed the question of the truth of what Jesus claimed to remain in the forefront. In all the confusion of arrest and accusations, of the smell, dust, heat, and noise of the crowd, this crucial matter did not get lost. God's purpose was achieved: Is what this man claims true?

Jesus' refusal to resist arrest and his refusal to have his disciples fight to save him enabled Pilate to realize that the truth of what Jesus claimed was the real issue between Jesus and his accusers — not sedition or treason. Jesus' behavior did not allow the threat of a cruel death by crucifixion deflect the focus of attention. In all the confusion of history and the noise of life around us, this question still comes through today: Is what he claimed true?

Jesus, then, was a particular kind of victim of injustice. To keep the crucial issue in the forefront by a commitment to God was an active, not a passive, role. He faced death and died in such a way that people are forced to face the important questions of life. We are so familiar with Jesus' trial and death that we frequently miss this feature. To highlight it, I will briefly examine the death of Socrates, which is not as familiar. By a comparison, the greatness of what is familiar will be easier to see.

At his trial, Socrates was accused of three things: atheism, leading young people astray (no doubt Alcibiades was especially in mind), and endangering the security of Athens. Those who brought the charges demanded the death penalty. This punishment was ridiculously severe. The jury of five hundred citizens would have been happy to close the whole affair with a minor fine. According to Athenian law, the jury had to choose between the alternatives proposed by the plaintiff and the defendant. Socrates' friends begged him to propose a fine, and even offered to pay it for him. But Socrates refused. He had obeyed a divine call to awaken his city to its ignorance and its need to search for a truer way to live. He said that he was of course only a minor person in the great city of Athens, no more than a gadfly, stinging a large beast in order to make it take notice of the way it was stumbling along, heedless of its direction. To carry out this mission, he had neglected his own business affairs. Now, as an old man, he was poor. He therefore proposed that the city provide him with a pension in recognition of his services.

The jury had to decide between the death penalty and a pension for services. The majority were so outraged with Socrates for making the situation so awkward that it voted for the death penalty. Everyone expected that while in prison, Socrates would come to his senses and admit that he was wrong. The city officials tried to arrange for Socrates to escape, but he refused to cooperate: Either I have been a benefactor and should receive a pension, or my accusers are right.

The jury had not reckoned on the seriousness of this little citizen; it was amazed at his passionate love of truth and at his deep commitment to the well-being of his fellow citizens. By his refusal to back down, even in the face of death, Socrates forced his fellow-citizens to face a vital issue. Is the basis of life to go unexamined? Are we just to stumble along? Will the gods allow this to go unpunished? If he had accepted a minor fine, or, when he saw that they meant business, escaped from prison, people would have been able to slide over these questions and continue to live untroubled but superficial lives.

By accepting a grossly unjust death, Socrates did not allow the people of his city to continue to live the way they wanted to live scot-free, but only at the price of the death of a wise, generous citizen who had devoted his life to their betterment. To be his kind of victim is not something that just happens. Socrates' and Jesus' deaths differed from those of countless victims of injustice because of the way they conducted themselves. Each of them suffered from injustice in such a way that he caused people to face the big questions of life.

There is, however, a very great difference between their deaths. In Jesus' death, God takes into himself the consequences of our evil. That is, he does not destroy us for the disobedience that harms ourselves and others. He does not try to win us over with bribes of earthly gain. He simply takes our rejection and turns it into something holy. The word "sacrifice" is made up of the Latin words "sacred or holy" and "to do or to make." God takes our rejection, rebellion, hatred, and indifference that leads to a judicial murder and makes it a holy act. The Father is able to do this because of the way the Son dies — willingly — for our sakes, making it clear in the way he dies that he dies for our sins.

George Herbert in his poem "The Agony" expresses this dual character of a judicial murder that is at the same time a holy action.

> Philosophers have measur'd mountains,
> Fathom'd the depths of seas, of states, and kings,
> Walk'd with a staff to heav'n, and traced fountains:
>   But there are two vast, spacious things,
> The which to measure it doth more behove:
> Yet few there are that sound them: Sin and Love.
>
> Who would know Sin, let him repair
> Unto Mount Olivet; there shall he see
> A man so wrung with pains, that all his hair,
>   His skin, his garments bloody be.
> Sin is that press and vice, which forceth pain
> To hunt his cruel food through ev'ry vein.
>
> Who knows not Love, let him assay
> And taste that juice, which on the cross a pike
> Did set abroach; then let him say
>   If ever he did taste the like.
> Love is that liquour sweet and most divine,
> Which my God feels as blood; but I as wine.[3]

Herbert tells us that if you want to know what sin is, look at that man on the cross. If you want to know what love is, look at the same place, to that man on the cross. Only God can make a cruel, unjust death into something holy, so that sin, which brings ruin upon us, and love, which redeems us, are to be found in the same place, united in Jesus.

Herbert makes it clear that the rejection of Christ in the crucifixion is not able to defeat God's love. God raises Jesus from the dead and the resurrected Lord comes back to us asking us to receive his love. It is as if God says to us in Jesus' resurrection: You cannot get rid of me. I keep coming back, even from the dead. Now what are you going to do about my love that continues to seek you?

---

3. George Herbert, *The Temple,* ed. John N. Wall, Jr. (New York: Paulist Press, 1981), p. 151.

VI. What Are We to Do about Jesus' Resurrection?

Ludwig Wittgenstein, perhaps the greatest philosopher of the twentieth century, left some of his personal reflections about Jesus' resurrection. They are to be found in one of his private notebooks, which has recently been printed under the title *Culture and Value.* The entry is in the year 1937. He wrote,

> What inclines even me to believe in Christ's resurrection? . . .
> — If he did not rise from the dead, then he decomposed in the grave like any other man. *He is dead and decomposed.* In that case he is a teacher like any other and can no longer *help;* and once again we are orphaned and alone. So we have to content ourselves with wisdom and speculation. We are in a sort of hell where we can do nothing but dream, roofed in, as it were, and cut off from heaven. But if I am to be REALLY saved, — what I need is *certainly* — not wisdom, dreams or speculation — and this certainty is faith. And faith is faith in what is needed by my *heart,* my *soul,* not my speculative intelligence. For it is my soul with its passions, as it were with its flesh and blood, that has to be saved, not my abstract mind. Perhaps we can say: Only *love* can believe the Resurrection. Or: it is *love* that believes even in the Resurrection; hold fast even to the Resurrection. What combats doubt is, as it were, *redemption.* Holding fast to *this* must be holding fast to that belief. . . . So this can come about only if you no longer rest your weight on the earth but suspend yourself from heaven. Then *everything* will be different and it will be "no wonder" if you can do things that you cannot do now. (A man who is suspended looks the same as one who is standing, but the interplay of forces within him is nevertheless quite different, so that he can act quite differently than can a standing man.)[4]

And once again, I think, the issue has been put before us clearly. For all we ever do is witness. A witness is one who puts the issue clearly. The issue is whether we stand on earth on our own feet or are suspended from above, attached to the living Lord.

---

4. *Culture and Value,* ed. G. H. von Wright, trans. Peter Winch (Oxford: Blackwell, 1980), p. 6e.

Epilogue: Wherever Two or Three Are Gathered Together

GARETH JONES

"LET US OFFER to God acceptable worship." The words are from the twelfth chapter of the letter to the Hebrews. Worship is something to which the author of this letter exhorts us to pay close attention. Let us be grateful, he implies, for receiving a kingdom that cannot be shaken; let us offer to God acceptable worship with reverence and awe. The verse underlines the crucial importance of public worship, and I would like to consider some of its dimensions here — three in particular.

The first is persistence. Worship possesses a uniquely stubborn character. It refuses to die out. Within the Judeo-Christian tradition, it has survived right up to the present time under the most adverse conditions. The Hebrew scriptures show that worship was an integral part of ancient Israelite society. The system of sacrifice practiced in Solomon's Temple was so significant that when the Temple was destroyed by Nebuchadnezzar, the exiled Jews were convinced that they no longer had access to God. "By the waters of Babylon," wrote the psalmist, "we sat down and wept when we remembered Zion." On the willows there, we hung up our harps, the superfluous instruments of worship. But despite this pessimism, Jewish worship not only continued but took on a new lease of life and eventually found a place in the synagogue, where it has survived against tremendous odds until this day.

In the story of Christian origins, in the book of Acts, for example, prominence is given to the survival of worship in the face of cruel persecution. When Christians began to experience life under Islam several centuries later, they found that they were greatly restricted in their witness. It was forbidden, for example, to display any Christian symbol outside a church building. To this day, churches in Muslim countries are not marked by a cross. It was forbidden to ring bells loudly, which is why such churches still have wooden clappers to call the faithful to prayer. Christians were often subject to punitive taxation, but they were allowed to worship. It is no accident that the Eastern Orthodox churches regard the litany as a supremely important part of the church's life. Maybe this is why it takes so long. In many countries, worship is all that some churches have been permitted as a witness to their faith, and they make the most of it.

The church in my home parish in Wales is dated A.D. 630. The present building stands on the site of the first mud hut erected by an itinerant monk who came our way in the seventh century — the Age of the Saints, as we call it. It is one of the many churches that dot the western seaboard of Britain and Ireland, testimonies to the existence of early Christian communities established when the Celts ruled the waves. Despite repeated raids by Vikings, the Celtic worshipping communities not only endured the so-called Dark Ages, they also flourished and made a significant contribution to the propagation of Christianity, in the British Isles and even in mainland Europe.

In our own time, in spite of repeated attempts by atheistic governments such as those of China and Eastern Europe to proscribe its expression, the instinct to worship has survived. Perhaps the most significant example is the celebration of Passover in Auschwitz. But this persistence, of course, is not only illustrated in the history books, it is also a very real dimension of contemporary church life. I don't know the story of this cathedral, but I believe it's safe to say that no Sunday has passed since the building was consecrated when the doors have not been open for worship. Various projects and programs, all of them worthwhile, have come and gone in response to the needs of the moment. But worship has remained. Whatever this place stands for, whatever it does or doesn't do, it will always sound the call to worship.

The importance of such continuity and worship is perhaps nowhere more clearly seen than in an interregnum when the congregation through its lay representatives strives to maintain, sometimes with difficulty, the regular round of prayer and praise. Such persistence must surely indicate that worship has a hold on something very deep in the human psyche — possibly because it points beyond the narrow limits of sight, touch, hearing, and deduction to the immeasurable arena of the spirit; possibly because it testifies to the eternal dimension in our Maker and to the hunger in our souls. However we perceive its significance, it surely answers a need; otherwise, I don't think it would have survived.

Worship is also about participation. The author of Hebrews was writing to a very dispirited group of people, to people who had all but given up trying to fight the paganism of the Roman Empire. He was writing to people who were on the point of renouncing their newfound faith and going with the tide. Originally, this letter was a rope thrown out to drifters to bring them back to shore. One of the criticisms the author levels at his readers is their neglect of public worship. In chapter 10 he says: "We ought to see how each of us may best arouse others to love and active service, not staying away from our meetings, as some do, but rather encouraging one another." This is a slap in the face, perhaps, for those who tend to skip the eight o'clock.

He returns to the same theme in chapter 12, and exhorts the Hebrews to pay greater attention to acceptable worship. By stressing the importance of the *congregation,* the author underlines the dangers of isolationism. He realizes that falling away from the fellowship of worship is the first step in falling away from the fellowship of faith.

The famous evangelist D. L. Moody once called on a leading Chicago businessman to talk about Christian commitment. They were seated in the parlour with a coal fire and drink. The man insisted that he need not join the church to be a Christian. He could be just as committed outside the fellowship of believers and worshippers as he could be within it. Moody listened in silence. When the man had finished speaking, Moody stepped to the fireplace and took a burning coal from the flames with a pair of tongs, then set it aside by itself in the grate. The coal of course smoldered and soon died out. Moody's host took the point and became an active churchman.

This truth, that faith implies a fellowship of like-minded people, worshipping people, is corroborated time and again in the Scriptures. It is almost always a *community* that God summons to serve him — not separate individuals, not prize specimens only. In the Old Testament, we hear of a *covenant* community — the chosen people. In the New Testament, we read of local churches in Corinth, Ephesus, Troas. It would never occur to a Jew or Christian that one could cut oneself off from the religious community and worship on one's own. There were no lone Christians, no isolated believers. Christianity and isolation is seldom a practical proposition. Worship implies participation, in the sense of belonging to a group. But of course it also implies participation in the more obvious sense of *joining in*.

This is nothing new for Anglicans. In the Middle Ages, however, the congregation was little more than a spectator group, a listening group — listening to the ceremonies enacted in the sanctuary. The fact that everything was in Latin did not encourage participation. But our Anglican forebears changed all that. They brought the congregation back into worship by dropping Latin in favour of English, by introducing hymns, eventually, and by encouraging everyone to take communion. As Episcopalians, as Anglicans, we are proud of this legacy. It's gratifying to see that the Roman Catholics have at last caught up with us. They would not listen to our pleas for the vernacular four hundred years ago; but now, they will have nothing else. In the wake of Vatican II, Polish, Japanese, and even Welsh replaced Latin overnight.

Third, there's the matter of propriety. Although I may have given the impression that I took the phrase "acceptable worship" to mean worship that was acceptable to *us,* this of course is not what the phrase means. The author of Hebrews is speaking of what is acceptable to *God.* This becomes clear in other translations. "Let us worship in a manner well pleasing to God." "Let us worship God as he would be worshipped." But the correct interpretation doesn't make the issue any easier to handle, for whether we like it or not, there is inevitably a subjective element in all this. That is, we deem to be acceptable to God what is acceptable to *us.* If *we* like it, then we assume that God likes it.

For the Russian Orthodox, the litany is not worth having unless it lasts three hours. The Salvation Army insists on turning everything into a kind of hymn sandwich. The Southern Baptist feels cheated if the sermon lasts less than 40 minutes and is not about sin. It soon becomes obvious that what is acceptable or proper in worship varies greatly. This highly subjective element contributes to making public worship a veritable minefield for those whose business it is to order it. In no other area is it easier to believe that our personal whims are fundamental principles. We all consider ourselves to be litanists. We can't claim perhaps to be Old Testament experts because we skipped those Hebrew classes we should have taken long ago. Since our Greek is a little rusty, we cannot claim New Testament expertise either. We might consider ourselves church historians until we are stumped on the date of the Second Crusade. But litany is different. We are all expert litanists.

If you don't believe me, apply a simple test. Try introducing new hymns or a different translation of the Bible. Or, God forbid, try revising the prayer book. Watch the hackles rise. Watch the experts coming out of the woodwork. Every parish priest has a whole host of consultants ever ready to advise on liturgical matters. For this reason, worship is a very emotional issue. People can sulk indefinitely if their concept of proper worship is undermined. They will even withdraw their membership and go and be a pain in the neck somewhere else. To my mind, there is a streak of arrogance in an attitude that says of worship, "If it isn't exactly to my taste, I'm justified in feeling aggrieved and kicking up a fuss."

Now this doesn't mean, of course, that we should accept uncritically what we genuinely believe to be substandard and sloppy. The propriety of worship requires careful monitoring, if for no other reason than the fact that it's the shop window of the church. What happens in a church on a Sunday can determine whether or not the casual visitor comes back. People looking for a spiritual home do not drop in at the men's breakfast or the altar guild meeting or matins on Thursday. They arrive at 10 o'clock on a Sunday morning. In terms of growth and mission, every congregation has sixty minutes to make it or mar it. There has to be something in every act of worship — and you will all have your own ideas as to what it is — which elicits the response, "That was a meaningful service. I'm going to come back."

So the worship you find acceptable and therefore assume is acceptable to God has several dimensions. It's marked by persistence. There's a long and enduring tradition of which you are heirs. It's marked by participation. You can't worship in isolation. And it's marked by propriety. The litany must be celebrated with a sense of order and reverence. As you no doubt remember, it was in the context of congregational worship that Christ promised to be present with his followers. "Where two or three" or two hundred or three hundred "are gathered together in my name, there am I in the midst of them."

When all is said and done, I suppose, nothing else really matters.

DATE DUE